Praise for *The Magic of Tiny Busi.*

"This is the best business book I've ever read. It's *Essentialism* and *Start with Why* meet *Good to Great* with a sensibility for the way life actually unfolds."
—**Caroline Duell, founder and CEO, All Good**

"Sharon shows us the magic that unfolds when we use business to serve us and are not servants to it."
—**Rose Penelope L. Yee, CEO, Green Retirement, Inc.**

"*The Magic of Tiny Business* is a compelling story of true entrepreneurship that is relatable, inspiring, and full of simple, practicable steps to living your desired business journey."
—**Henry Cross, Executive Director, Hosh Yoga and Hosh Kids**

"There's nothing tiny about the vision behind this inspirational book that's part memoir and part how-to guide for dreamers who yearn to be doers and start up their own businesses. Authentic, transparent, and funny at times. So if you're itching to do something with your life that lights up your passion and provides a paycheck, settle in for a good read."
—**Sandra Ann Harris, founder of ECOlunchbox**

"Sharon challenges the Wall Street mindset. This is an inspiring book for all entrepreneurs looking to embrace an alternative paradigm—where tiny businesses are sustainable, purpose-driven, and successful."
—**Nona Lim, founder and CEO, Nona Lim Foods**

"'Begin with your life in mind' is the mantra that drives this book. The magic of the tiny business approach is the intentional commitment to grow our companies in a way that supports the quality of our lives."
—**Ellen Ornato, Founding Partner, The Bolder Company**

"*The Magic of Tiny Business* is a practical, hands-on guide to launching and running an impact business (so your business doesn't run you)."
—**Denise Taschereau and Sarah White, cofounders of Fairware**

"The writing is an appealing mix of Zen-like wisdom and practical, actionable business advice. The overall effect is honest, human, useful . . . food for thought, a manifesto for action, and a blueprint for success in one book!"
—**Jonathan Peck, Dovetail Publishing Services**

"Craft the life you want—with a business to support it. It's the message we all need to hear."
—**Susan Danziger, founder and CEO, Ziggeo.com**

"Rowe proves it is not only okay to prioritize a high quality of life *and* an honorable vocation, but it is exactly this magic combination that makes it all worthwhile."
—**Shawn Berry, cofounder/worker-owner, LIFT Economy**

"If you're an entrepreneur, founder, or aspiring leader, Sharon Rowe will remind you why you love business and how much good you can do in the world—at any size."
—**Corey Blake, founder and CEO, Round Table Companies**

"Sharon shows you how to have a beautiful business that is a blessing to your staff and your community no matter how big or how small it may be."
—**Dr. Judith Wright, coauthor of *The Heart of the Fight***

"A definitive book. Tiny business is big business!"
—**Karen Sands, MCC, BCC, leading GeroFuturist, bestselling author, thought leader, and speaker**

"*The Magic of Tiny Business* is a welcome invitation to rethink how business is built and how we define success."
—**Jessica Quinn, Managing Director, Civic Hall**

"Rowe's book is a refreshing perspective on entrepreneurship, reminding both new and experienced founders to take a deeper look at what it means to be successful, happy, and impactful in our work."
—**Desiree Vargas Wrigley, founder of Pearachute**

"*The Magic of Tiny Business* confronts the fears commonly faced by entrepreneurs who strive to change the status quo. Sharon Rowe shares pearls of wisdom on how to zero in on the mission while maintaining a balanced lifestyle."
—**Alisa Gravitz, President and CEO, Green America**

"In the constant-swirling mind of a business owner, Sharon's words are calming and a reminder of how to focus on what's important and define success in our own terms."
—**Rebecca Rodskog, cofounder of FutureLeaderNow and founder of 12@12**

The Magic of
Tiny Business

The Magic of Tiny Business

You Don't Have to Go Big to
Make a Great Living

Sharon Rowe

Illustrations by Julian Rowe

Berrett–Koehler Publishers, Inc.
a BK Business book

Berrett-Koehler Publishers, Inc.
1333 Broadway, Suite 1000
Oakland, CA 94612-1921
Tel: (510) 817-2277
Fax: (510) 817-2278
www.bkconnection.com

ORDERING INFORMATION

Quantity sales. Special discounts are available on quantity purchases by corporations, associations, and others. For details, contact the "Special Sales Department" at the Berrett-Koehler address above.

Individual sales. Berrett-Koehler publications are available through most bookstores. They can also be ordered directly from Berrett-Koehler: Tel: (800) 929-2929; Fax: (802) 864-7626; www.bkconnection.com.

Orders for college textbook/course adoption use. Please contact Berrett-Koehler: Tel: (800) 929-2929; Fax: (802) 864-7626.

Distributed to the U.S. trade and internationally by Penguin Random House Publisher Services.

Berrett-Koehler and the BK logo are registered trademarks of Berrett-Koehler Publishers, Inc.

Printed in the United States of America

Berrett-Koehler books are printed on long-lasting acid-free paper. When it is available, we choose paper that has been manufactured by environmentally responsible processes. These may include using trees grown in sustainable forests, incorporating recycled paper, minimizing chlorine in bleaching, or recycling the energy produced at the paper mill.

Cataloging-in-Publication Data is available at the Library of Congress.

ISBN: 978-1-5230-9478-3

First Edition
25 24 23 22 21 20 19 18   10 9 8 7 6 5 4 3 2 1

Interior design and production: Dovetail Publishing Services
Cover designer: Wes Youssi, M.80 Design

**Dedicated to my family, who inspires
me daily: Blake, Julian, and Eva**

This book is for those who want to build a profitable business on their own terms by doing work that is meaningful—and still be home for dinner with family and friends.

Contents

Preface

Here's the thing: If you're like most of us, you need to work and make a living. But more than that, you *want* to be part of something, to contribute, and to add value. You want to make a great living doing something you stand for. You may not know exactly all of what you want, but you know a lot about what you *don't* want.

What each of us needs and wants might look different, but there are common threads. I'm going to guess that you want:

Time: the freedom to choose when and how to use your time

Resources: the money to support yourself now and in the future

Relationships: people to share your life with

Meaning: the knowledge that what you do matters

Maybe you're thinking of starting a business but the whole thing is overwhelming. I'm sure you have your reasons why it seems like too much—no money, no time, and no know-how are the usual culprits. I'm here to tell you that even if you start with nothing (by the way, nobody really starts with nothing) but your purpose and patience, you can build something substantial, measurable, and worthwhile. In this book I will pass along some advice, guidelines, and access to community to help you get started.

Why not make your work life work for you—with a return? Why not build something *and* live the life you imagine? I'm not talking about finding fame and fortune through business. Not everyone wants that. I didn't. I'm directing you to a happy middle ground I call Tiny Business where business rules and personal choices are woven and work together from your center.

Just to be clear, this is not a book about having a one-person business that some might describe as "tiny." My definition of "tiny" has more to do with intention and purpose than size or income. Tiny refers to your focus on the essentials—and the compromises you won't make. My Tiny Business, Eco-Bags Products, does on average $2 million in sales annually. I also consider Patagonia, with over $200 million in revenue, to be a Tiny Business because it is so committed to its purpose.

Tiny Business, Big Purpose

Have you heard of the Tiny House movement? It is the growing trend of people intentionally downsizing their living spaces for a number of reasons, and the one that seems to resonate the most is the freedom and time that efficient and purposeful Tiny living brings.

Purpose Brings Meaning and Happiness

Like a Tiny House, a Tiny Business is built by keeping a laser focus on what you deem essential and eliminating what's nonessential—all the extra stuff. Tiny House advocates say it's about creating and living an intentional life with less. The first step is deciding when to say no. You have to get tough on what to include and what to throw out. By identifying what's important and essential, you make it easier to eliminate physical and mental clutter and experience life—and business—with greater ease and more abundance.

A Tiny Business is defined by your priorities and intentions, not how many employees you have. It has everything to do with your level of focus and not just how much revenue you bring in. It recognizes that growth is good—but not growth at all costs.

A Tiny Business approach takes a long view. It requires a disciplined mindset that breaks down problems into opportunities and encourages taking incremental, deliberate steps to keep you and your business healthy and vital.

This book is the story of my Tiny Business, Eco-Bags Products. It's about how I built a niche brand to solve a problem I was passionate about with persistence and patience, from a single idea, with very limited resources. It's how I intentionally grew a Tiny Business from a tiny idea into a profitable multimillion-dollar operation at my own pace, while prioritizing family and vacations.

Yes, you don't have to scrape by or sacrifice everything to make a great living!

Yes, you can build a profitable, million-dollar Tiny Business without working weekends and nights!

It can be done!

Tiny Business Is Business within Reach

But don't get me wrong: it's not easy. Building a Tiny Business requires great agility, creativity, and discipline. With decisions to be made at every turn, standing for something bigger than (but including) profit presents interesting challenges. That's what makes articulating your "why"—a clear and simple vision for what you want to create in life, business, and the world—so important. Tiny Business is about setting your intentions to create value and impact now—and for the future.

> **"**
>
> ***When you take the time to get very clear on what you want, choose a direction, and remove all obstacles, you'll find yourself moving with a greater sense of ease and freedom, creating a kind of "magic."***
>
> **"**

I'm defining "magic" as the freedom and joy you experience when you combine exquisite focus and consistent effort over time. When you know exactly what you want, it makes it easy to push everything you don't want—all the clutter and noise—to the wayside.

Tiny Business Is Business on Your Terms—That Fits Your Life

Entrepreneurship doesn't need to be a competitive race to the peak, as popular myths and media want you to believe. It can be a pleasurable, educational hike, from point A to point B, step by step to the summit, where you arrive in healthier financial and personal shape than when you began. With a Tiny Business, you get to stop and smell the flowers (and have fun) along the way. You eventually get where you're going, and you're more whole when you get there.

Introduction

Almost thirty years ago, when my acting career filled seats but not my bank account and new responsibilities arrived in the form of a baby, I needed to change direction. I wanted to put my family first, generate a good income, and do something that would make an impact. I didn't want the pressure that comes with a competitive position and a dictated work schedule. Jobs in the corporate world with windows (and doors!) that never opened felt deadening to me. I naively thought it would be easier to start something myself.

I Call Myself a Reluctant Entrepreneur

Find success, take charge of my own schedule, and make money—as easy as 1-2-3!

I grew up in a retail family business: Milt's Army and Navy in Bloomfield, Connecticut. My father worked long hours, and I began working there when I was twelve—missing, by the way, every Saturday high school event, including the football games. I knew I didn't want *that* kind of business. Not for me!

I wanted something else, something that didn't exist yet, at least not to my knowledge. I wanted to have a voice, a way to share my ideas, contribute, make a good living, and manage my own time. I didn't want to pay to play, meaning I was unwilling to make compromises to work up the corporate ladder. I didn't want to sacrifice the present for the future. I understood that time is precious, that it is the one resource we can't make more of. I wanted to build something and have time to play while doing it. I was tired of making compromises. And so, as an experienced actor with years of dealing with rejections, I figured, "Why not?" Why not do my own thing?

I had an idea. A "tiny" idea that excited me. I wanted to introduce the concept of reusable shopping bags like the ones I'd seen in France years earlier. I was tired of single-use plastic bags and figured other people were probably tired of them too. They always broke. They got stuck in trees and gutters. Instant garbage. So wasteful. They didn't make practical or environmental sense. When I saw them littering the streets it made me sad and mad. I believed then, and still do, that access to a clean environment, air, and water is a human right.

I was an actor and a new mom married to a freelance musician living in a big city where making a living isn't easy or optional. Even with manageable rent it was a financial stretch. I made choices, designating strict working hours and healthy, reasonable income goals. I made up business rules to support my environmental goals (leave no trace) and social priorities (fair wages for fair labor). I diligently researched and picked the first suppliers who were a good match. They weren't perfect, but I needed to get started.

*"I know, sweetie, but the environment
doesn't make daddy any money."*

Choices available to me:

Family/home + work 9–5 (away all day) + commuting
+ home late = exhausted

vs.

Choices I made:

Work from home + 1099s + flex childcare + flex hours
+ extra hours = more relaxed every
day

What I did was very practical on many levels:

1. *I found something I was passionate about (my "why").*

   I was determined to rid the world of its single-use plastic bag habit and make my living doing it.

2. *I started a business that was a solution to a problem (more of my "why").*

I manufactured and sold a responsibly made, environmental lifestyle product to replace wasteful, environmentally unfriendly plastic bags.

3. *I used my own resources (my "how").*

I bootstrapped using my own savings. I hit the streets and juggled credit cards for cash flow. I made it up as I went along. I made a lot of mistakes, and I learned what I needed.

What was less practical? I built a company from scratch with no formal business training. I didn't wait to create a master business plan. I jumped in, willing to take a long view.

I had a vision for cleaning up the planet and making a very good living without selling my soul. I made up my own rules guided by my own sense of what was important for my business and my young family. Without a backup plan or the luxury of time, I figured out how to create sustainable growth and healthy profits without big business plans and big capital—and without working 24/7.

And in addition to building a healthy, profitable enterprise, my Tiny Business helped me:

- Set a good example
- Attract the best people to work with me
- Enjoy the work that I do
- Grow in community versus in isolation
- Inspire others
- Build the life I imagine

Isn't that what we all want?

> *"Pick yourself."*
> —Seth Godin

I bet on me, and I believe you should bet on you.

If you have what some think are conflicting ideas—you want your work to matter and you want to make a good living, or you want to build your own business while keeping family and other life experiences a priority—then a Tiny Business is for you.

If your measure of success is making a good enough income to lead a rich life and being able to do what you want when you want to do it, then what I share in this book will resonate.

I'm writing this because I know the magic that happens when you get very clear on the life you want and you take deliberate, disciplined, informed steps to create it—when you create a Tiny Business.

Tiny Business Is Business on YOUR Terms—That Fits YOUR Life

I. It is driven by consciously chosen limitations that increase your focus on the things that matter. *Tiny means how to say no.*

II. This focus helps you prioritize your "why"—the things that matter to you and that you want to create—in life, business, and the world.

III. These priorities guide every decision in your "how"— the business realities and practices that get things done.

IV. Focus, priorities, and clarity create a magic that let you enjoy the process. You remember to breathe, and you thrive through it all. *Tiny means how to say yes.*

The Magic of Tiny Business encompasses all the lessons I learned and the time-tested Tiny Business insights and advice I want to share so that you can have a smoother journey.

In part I, I go deeper into what a Tiny Business is and what it means to consciously choose your limitations—whether it's leaving work at 5:00 p.m. every day without fail, having a positive environmental impact, or enjoying a flexible schedule. I help you take inventory of what you have to start with (trust me, it's enough!), what you will need going forward, and the steps you can take to get it.

Part II is about getting clear on your "why." What do you want for your life, your business, and the world? Why do you want to start your own business? Why are you passionate about selling this particular product or service? Breaking down the answers to these questions will help you get clear on your brand and your story—the unique value you are adding to the marketplace.

In part III, I get into the nitty-gritty of starting and growing a Tiny Business—from cash flow to accounting and anticipating growth and slowdowns—all the while keeping your "why" front and center.

Part IV is about keeping *you* whole throughout the process. A Tiny Business is about making a good living and a great life. You need to be able to stop and smell the flowers, or get a glass of water, or take a walk when you feel like it—you need to enjoy the journey. This section shows you how.

This is not an exhaustive guide to creating and sustaining a Tiny Business, but it does highlight some of the key and creative approaches that worked for me. In every chapter, you will find takeaways with guidelines and guardrails from my own Tiny Business journey. I include advice on how to navigate and use the noise to your best advantage, and how to leverage being in a community and standing for something. I share best practices on working collaboratively, managing growth, and managing cash. I may even be the bug in your ear that keeps you going when you want to quit, though quitting can be a good way to reconnect with what you want. More on that later.

I share my mistakes in the hope that I can spare you from making the same ones. But trust me, you will find others!

And if (when?) you do skin your knees along the way, remember that it's only skin. And when you've got skin in the game, you stick with it.

Part I

Choose Your Limitations

This Won't Hurt a Bit . . .

Chapter One

What Is a Tiny Business?

"

*Go big or go home is a prevailing but
tired and misleading cultural myth.*

"

Risk everything. Don't even bother to try otherwise.

Fight your way to the top.

Be aggressive.

And If You Don't Succeed . . .

You're done.

You're ruined.

You lose.

You'll never be successful.

No one wants to be your friend (aww).

Have I scared you? Going big is not for everyone. It wasn't for me—not like that.

But what if someone asked you: What sparks, excites, invigorates, or inspires you?

And what if I showed you a way to be different in business that also led to success? A way that allowed you to take one step at a time instead of risking everything all at once while leaping into the unknown? A way that lets you intentionally build what you want, going slow and steady, and only picking up the pace when you're ready?

You can have your cake and eat it too. With a Tiny Business, you can make a good living and have a great life.

What a Tiny Business Is

1. Born out of crystal-clear priorities for what you want out of life.

2. Makes you a living and still gives you the space to live.

3. Puts your energy into something that matters exquisitely to you.

4. Grows at your own pace and in alignment with your life priorities.

5. Business on your terms—that fits your life.

What a Tiny Business Is Not

1. Born solely out of the need for a paycheck.

2. Requires you to push aside everything else important in your life.

3. Puts all your energy into making money.

4. Grows for the sake of growth without consideration for your other life priorities.

5. Business on business's terms—that you have to work your life around.

Building Market Value with YOUR Values

Tiny is a laser-focused, disciplined approach centered on making your work work for you. It is rooted in your priorities and supported with tested business acumen. It's a way to start, run, and grow a business where you can stand for something and create a scalable working asset without working 24/7. Tiny Business is a big opportunity; it's your opportunity to drive the bus. You get to build market value with your values.

66

Tiny does not define the amount of revenue you generate—that can be as big as your aspirations.

99

Like the Tiny House movement, the first step is getting clear on your priorities. What do you want in your life and your business now and with an eye toward the future? Like a Tiny House, there are things you need to have and things that are nice to have. If your Tiny Business is a journey and you have one small bag to pack for one full year, what needs to be in it?

What's most important to you?

What are you working for really?

What is your "why"?

> **"**
> *Tiny Business is how you make*
> *a living, not a killing.*
> **"**

With a Tiny mindset, you start with what's most important, both personally and professionally, and you regularly visit those priorities for all decisions. You practice discipline by setting a schedule, sticking to it, and getting to work. You build something you are connected to—emotionally, psychologically, and physically—something that feeds your energy.

You select what's essential and then you intentionally remove the obstacles, noise, and clutter—real or imagined. You consciously limit your business and your life to only what you need and want. This is how you create and live an intentional life with less.

> *"Rich . . . It's about having enough*
> *money to live your best life."*
>
> —Amy Adeyemi, Toro Communications

What I wanted was

- A flexible schedule
- Nights and weekends free plus at least four weeks of vacation
- To put my family first (e.g., not missing school plays)
- Time for self-care (daily swim and meditation)

- Financial security
- To believe in what I'm doing 100 percent
- To solve a problem without creating new ones

Yes, I wanted it all. It took a lot of work and a lot of discipline, and I got it.

Tiny Business is serious business. It's complex. It's not an easy, by-any-means-possible, get-rich-quick approach. It is weighted in your values and takes a long view requiring patience and persistence. But once you get clear on what you want, commit to it, and roll up your sleeves, you will begin to see the abundance of resources available to support you and connect you to a like-minded community.

What Matters Most To You?

Here's a picture that maybe describes you . . .

You've got an itch to do something bigger, but you also need to make a living. There's probably a lot of fear around changing things up, depending on what (and who) you're responsible for. I'm certain there's a lot of excitement bubbling around your passion too. Tiny Business is an opportunity to embrace and focus this energy to support you.

If you feel like you're ready to start but you can't put your finger on what's stopping you, that means you need to take a break and unpack what you're asking of yourself.

Start with what you want in life and work.

◆ Time and money to travel

◆ Coming home for dinner every night

◆ Bringing your dog to work

◆ Easy or no commute

◆ Working for a brand or business you believe in

If that doesn't feel comfortable, start with what you don't want.

◆ Limited vacation

◆ Forty-plus hour workweeks

◆ Working in a cubicle

◆ Long commute

◆ Spending your time on a brand or business you don't trust or believe in

Keep on adding to your lists.

Next, look at your relationships to critical business concepts. What is your understanding and experience of . . .

◆ Money

◆ Risk

◆ Profit

◆ Success

This stuff seems pretty basic and easy to tick off, but it is very loaded when you dive in.

Begin these conversations with yourself gently at first, but go deeper when you see yourself starting to move away. Do free writing.[1] Keep a journal or, if you're visual, sketch it out or make a collage. Nothing you write, say, draw, or compose will be wrong or right. This is the vulnerability needed to open up and spark what you really want for your life, your business, and the world. This is the foundation of a Tiny Business.

Challenge Your Assumptions

I'm suggesting you start a new and honest relationship with yourself to tackle important conceptual business blocks. Don't be lazy and settle for vague definitions or rely on what you think mainstream culture says.

For example, if you have no idea what "risk tolerance" means, then acknowledge that that's your relationship with this concept right now.

"

You don't need to know everything to start, but you must have a handle on what you know and don't know.

"

"Are we here yet?"

This is an ongoing process, which I learned the hard way.

Business concepts have deep cultural roots and can trigger very personal reactions. The tendency with unexamined concepts is to avoid thinking about them until absolutely necessary, then reacting emotionally when situations arise.

When situations arise and decisions need to be made, you want to be in the most prepared position possible in order to respond with well-thought-out responses. Start this work when you're not under pressure to respond to anything urgent, and trust that your understanding will grow with time.

Break It Down (Tiny Steps)

The lesson here is incrementalism: break everything down so there is meaning for you. It's about learning how to take tiny steps, starting a personal relationship with your concepts and challenging assumptions so you can pick your best path forward.

Here's where I started:

Money: I didn't have enough, couldn't seem to make enough, and didn't understand what I had—or did not have—access to. This made me feel very uncomfortable. I lied to friends, saying I couldn't go out because I was busy when really I was just broke. I quickly realized that with a business I would have to use and manage borrowed money (i.e., debt) for growth. This started my next conversation on risk.

Before you move to the next conversation, first answer these questions for yourself.

- Do you have money to invest in your business?
- Do you have access to money? If your answer is yes, list all the people and places you can get it and how much from each.
- What's your relationship to having or not having money?
- What's enough money?
- What's your stretch goal and what will it get you?

Business is currency for ideas.

—Me

Risk Tolerance: I had no real idea what my risk tolerance with money was. I'd failed plenty of auditions but those nicked my heart, not my bank account. Being asked to describe my tolerance for risk on a scale from 1 to 10 held no meaning to me. I didn't have anything to lose yet. Like a three-year-old skiing, I was close to the ground. Now, I work with forecasts to analyze and manage risk.

- Are you financially secure right now?
- If so, for how long?
- How much do you need now and three months from now?
- How much can you afford to lose or put toward an opportunity?
- What are you willing to risk being without right now?

Financial Security: Initially this meant paying basic bills plus a little extra for playing. Then it grew to include mortgage and tuition payments, savings, and access to credit. What stage are you in?

- What is the dollar amount on your monthly need to haves (essentials) versus want to haves (desires)?
- What does the space between those two figures tell you?
- How will your essentials and desires change over the next twelve months?

Profit: Don't consume it, use it.

I confused profit with compensation for years. I disregarded the sage advice of "pay yourself first," totally missing the point of rewarding yourself for your work, no matter the amount. After thirty years in business, I have learned to actively promote paying yourself first. You must put air in your tires or you won't be able to drive the car. But the amount you pay yourself is another discussion. Pick a percentage for your compensation: gross revenue minus your compensation minus expenses equals profit. Think of profit as the asset you can use to build your business.

- What's your current understanding and definition of profit?
- What are your expenses?
- What are you paying yourself?
- How can you use your profits to grow your business?

Success: Success for me meant having the resources for the experiences I wanted now and in the future. Flexibility and good health have been key, allowing for both camping and five-star hotel stays. Now, success includes having a platform and the time to share with an audience what I've learned. Practice painting a picture of what success looks like for you on a daily basis.

- Three years from now, what do you want success to look like?
- Think of yourself at age eighty. What has made your life successful?

The French Press Story

An old friend and I were talking about what it would be like to live on a boat for more than a week. She said, "So long as I have my French press, I'm good. No matter how wet, rocky, steamy, or smelly the boat gets, if I can have a hot cup of java from my French press in the morning, all is good in the world."

What's your French press, the one thing that can make you feel like everything is okay in the world?

Create a list of things that make you happy, no matter what.

Here's my list:

- Weekends to chill out and be with family and friends
- Beach weeks—it has to be more than a week

- Swimming every day in the summer
- Dinners by the river at sunset
- Buying food at the farmer's market
- Cooking at home
- The ability to buy things, regular things, when I need them (I'm okay with having to save for bigger items)
- Acting and going to the theater when I can
- Visiting friends
- Hiking
- Traveling, whether it's close to home or far away

Figure out what the essentials and desires are on your list. Make sure the essentials are part of your "why." And don't compromise.

Chapter Two

Work with What You've Got and Make It Work

❝

I didn't know everything I wanted, but I knew what I was unwilling to live with.

❞

One day after a nonstop morning of working from home for the job I had before I started my business, I stepped away from my desk to take a much-needed bio break. The phone rang and the answering machine picked it up.

Imagine hearing your manager's voice coming at you over the tiny speaker of your answering machine screaming how irresponsible you are because you are not exactly where he expects to find you at an exact moment in time. I had a newborn son, had coordinated day care so I could work from home, and took my responsibility for making a living and contributing to my new family's financial health and well-being seriously. I was one of his top-performing salespeople and the only woman on the team.

What I did next wasn't responsible or logical. I needed this job. I had been an actor and knew that wouldn't pay my bills on a regular basis. I had no backup plan and only a teensy bit of savings. Nevertheless, I called my supervisor back and told him I quit. He told me I couldn't. I did anyway.

> *"If you are passionate about solving a problem, you will learn any skill necessary to get the job done."*
>
> —Onyeka Obiocha, Director of Innovation, Yale University, Center for Public Service and Social Justice

I couldn't get another job-job (i.e., one that kills your soul to make a buck). Now was the time to make my tiny idea a real business. I had to make it work. That's the day Eco-Bags Products got started for real.

When asked how I started my business, I used to be very quick to say, "I started with nothing and made something." It sounded bold, and it placed me in the "rags to riches" myth category. But it was a lie. Not only was it not my truth, it perpetuated larger cultural myths around being an entrepreneur. I wasn't honest with myself, and I was misleading others.

What Do You Have? Something vs. Nothing

Over the years, I dug a little deeper into what I was calling "nothing" and discovered that I did, in fact, start with quite a few "somethings." When I added these insights to my conversations and public talks, my origin story became more relatable. And if I'd done a deeper dive, making this list when I first started, I would've been more grounded.

"

Nothing vs. Something
No things vs. Some things
Some vs. Sum

"

If you're hungry and creative, you can whip up a filling and delicious meal with whatever ingredients you have on hand. Starting out, I knew I didn't have everything I needed. We didn't have a lot in savings, wealthy relatives, or experience working with OPM (other people's money). So I had to be creative and adaptive with what I had on hand.

One thing I had was space—and I also had rent to pay and a baby to care for. So my husband and I found a roommate who was willing to help with childcare in exchange for reduced rent. That helped on two fronts. A roommate was not something we particularly wanted—it was decidedly outside the norm for a young family—but we needed a creative short-term solution to help pay the rent and for childcare as I worked on getting my business off the ground. We did what we needed to do.

Your Nothing Is Actually a Whole Lot of Somethings

When you start something, it's essential to be honest about what you have, what you don't have, and what you need to get. You need to put your personal "nothing" into perspective. Embrace what you have. Don't minimize or overblow it. It'll make you stronger.

Look deeply at what you have—whatever it is, it's what's in your tool kit. It is something to begin to work with, to add and improve on as you build your business. And by honestly evaluating what you have, you can more effectively and efficiently get what you need.

"

The sum of some is . . . enough.

"

Exercise: Take Inventory

Take inventory of what you have right now that could help you get your Tiny Business off the ground. I recommend that you make this list in at least two ways:

- The normal and comfortable way—for example, writing it out on pen and paper or your laptop
- An unusual and uncomfortable way—for example, writing left-handed if you're a righty (or vice versa)

The latter is a simple way to get you out of your comfort zone and thinking creatively. When you do something in a new or different way, you slow down. New thoughts and insights occur. If it feels silly or dumb, then you're doing it right!

However you do it, make this list today. It will give you a very clear picture of what you have to work with right now.

Here's my list of what I had when I started. Use it as a guide to create your own.

Family: A husband and a newborn son.

Housing: A two-bedroom apartment in New York City where rent was about a third of our income.

Education: A BA in liberal arts with a major in theater from a well-respected but not Ivy League university.

Friends: Lifelong friends, most living a phone call away.

Family income: My husband was a freelance musician and teacher.

Health insurance: Self-paid.

Skills: Acting and improvisation, sales, retail experience growing up, writing (I did a few low-pay writing gigs with local newspapers in NYC at one point).

Equipment: Landline phone, fax machine, Macintosh SE, and a printer. (This was pre-internet so no email, no Google, not even cell phones!)

Wealthy parents or in-laws: Nope

Trust fund: Are you kidding?

Savings: A teensy bit.

Good credit: Yes.

Access to credit: Yes (credit cards).

Business connections: Not really. My father had a small retail store I grew up in. I had some friends in video editing, which I thought wasn't applicable. My friends were all creatives: actors and teachers. I didn't think they knew anything more than me.

What Is Enough?

We all have a very complex relationship with money—having it, not having it, not having enough of it. There's never enough.

What I know now that I did not know when I quit my job is that you can't let money shape you. Instead, you need to use money to shape what you want. A close friend, Peter Berley, chef and cookbook author framed this for me years ago. He said:

"Money is energy. It's a tool."

After years of wrestling with it, I finally got money where it belonged: in my tool kit.

Don't get trapped into thinking it's all about the money. It's not always about the money. Tiny Business understands money as an asset, an energetic and necessary tool to building something. It's an essential piece in your tool kit, but it's not the only driver. And in the absence of money, you can become (and will have to be) a super-creative problem solver. Think of problems as the blank canvas for you, the entrepreneur.

Until you build a healthy relationship with how much money is enough for your life—what you need to live on versus what you want to live with—you will not be able to harness the energy of money and use it efficiently. You need to know your number, your personal financial baseline as well as what is needed for your Tiny Business.

What's the least amount you need to live and work with?

What's the least amount you can live and work with and still have some fun?

I recommend allocating 10 percent of your baseline toward savings (room to breathe) and 10 percent toward fun (room to live).

"

You can create something of substance from a tiny sum.

"

Who Do You Know? (And What Do They Know?)

You will read a lot in this book about the importance of relationships. When you're starting out, you may think you are independent but really you are interdependent.

Whether you're sparked to stay local with a community café or build an app for rounding up online purchases for nonprofit giving, you are part of a growing ecosystem of people who understand that business is a currency for ideas and for solving big problems. You can do good and do well at the same time—and you need skills and services that other folks have.

Research your favorite brands. Look for the ones that seem to share your values. Find their origin stories, the kernels that reveal their "whys," and look at how they started. Find what sparked them. Identify what you would like to keep for yourself and what you don't need or want.

Who are the people behind the businesses that are doing things differently, rooting their decisions in more than profit, and with an understanding that profit can be used as a force for good? Businesses like Eco-Bags Products were created and thrive at this intersection.

"Individually you can make a difference. Together we create an impact."

—Jeff Kirschner, Social Entrepreneur, Litterati

Thirty years ago, I worked in a vacuum. It was a challenge to simply get recycled copy paper and nontoxic inks, let alone flexible work hours. That was then. Now, I have a "tribe," as Seth Godin calls it.

There's an awake and enlightened group of business-people with a welcome mat at the door. It's a growing movement with the belief that when the tide rises, all boats rise. It's a space that's collaborative and competitive. It's a global movement of B Corps: business as a force for good.[1] Whether you want to grow and sell a Tiny Business or inspire other businesses with your actions, it's important to know you are not alone. Come join us.

> *"Never doubt that a small group of thoughtful,*
> *committed citizens can change the world;*
> *indeed, it's the only thing that ever has."*
>
> —Margaret Mead

Get the Lay of the Land

Who do you know who has a business that's like the one you want to start? If you don't know anyone personally, maybe you know someone in your city or town, or an internet acquaintance. Figure out what you're most curious about or in need of and ask if they have a few moments to spend with you.

Questions you can ask include:

◆ What inspired you to start?

◆ What motivates you?

◆ What was and is your financial picture?

◆ Where are you now versus where you want to be?

On a scale of 1 to 10, are you building your business on your own terms?

- What is your biggest obstacle to doing so?
- How many hours do you work per week?
- What does success mean to you?

If asking a local business owner questions seems too daunting or you cannot get their attention, look for meet-ups with businesspeople—for example, women in business associations, chamber of commerce events, or your local Rotary Club. Go with the intention of listening, with the possibility that you may (or may not) make a connection with someone.

Networking = Expanding your net and working it

Get to know the field you're playing in. Listen and learn the language of business, regardless of whether you want to play by the rules or make up your own. Go to local meet-ups. Talk to people you don't know and who don't know you. Have fun with it.

> *"One single real connection is what satisfies when I go to an event. I never know how that connection will play out but somehow it always does, in time."*
>
> —Hugh Locke, Social Business
> Entrepreneur, Smallholder Farmers
> Alliance—Haiti

Get Comfortable Being Uncomfortable

You may feel uncomfortable going to your first business event—like a total outsider. You are not the only person in the room who feels this way. Don't flee. Make yourself stay. Be consistent and show up at the same type of meeting on a regular basis. Just by showing up, you begin to weave yourself into the fabric of the community you want to be a part of.

If you know there's someone in the room you absolutely need to talk to but you haven't met, you can be freaked out or joyful. It's always a choice. If you have an intention to walk into the room and a practice to keep you grounded (like a mantra), you will be okay in the moment. Throw your shoulders back and say "I am the Queen of England" to yourself before you walk into the room. It works not only by giving you strength and focus to fulfill your agenda (e.g., meeting that essential person) but also by lightening things up.

Now try a different approach. Walk into the room with no agenda and know that you are interesting (enough) and that something you say will connect with another

"How about we just curl up inside and watch a movie?"

person. How can you do that? Ask an unusual question. Or do like my friend Drew: find someone standing alone, walk up to them, and say, "I don't know anyone. What brings you here?"

The more you walk into rooms without an agenda, the more comfortable you'll become walking into rooms.

Five Tips for Walking into a Room with Strangers

1. Make sure you're not thirsty or hungry or tired (ensure your physical body is satiated).
2. Pick a mantra or song to get you out of your head.
3. Take a few centering breaths and walk into the room.
4. Commit to listening versus talking.
5. Be curious.

Go to these meet-ups to learn, to find a community where you can exchange ideas, to find a place to land. Commit to talking to at least one person the first time and maybe two the next. Be prepared to talk about your idea in whatever shape it's in. Talk about as much of it as you're comfortable with or be expansive and make it all up. Listen and watch for what people are responding to. Is it your idea or your energy, or are they simply being polite?

If you're nervous someone will steal your idea, talk in the abstract until you're comfortable enough to share more details. My sense is that everyone has the same ideas at the same time anyway—if they're tuned in.

But not everyone has the interest or initiative to get started. Why not? Because not everyone knows what's in their tool kit to make it happen.

Part II

Let Your "Why" Speak

Prioritize and Focus Is the Tiny Way . . .

Chapter Three

Taking Tiny Steps

"

Cold and more than a little uncomfortable, I hit the streets to talk to people about my idea.

"

When hiking, "starting off cold" means, literally, starting off chilly, allowing for a little initial discomfort by not wearing all your layers because you'll warm up soon enough. A new concept may not feel right or ready, and the best way to find out if it has legs is simply to get started, even if you're cold, to take that first tiny step.

I had a tight three-month time window to see if I could make my Tiny Business idea work before I would have to look for a job-job. And so, without a business name, a business plan, or even a product to sell, I took my first step. I didn't know it then, but what I was doing was looking for people like me.

I was looking for a pulse.

I was curious if anyone else had traveled abroad and brought their own bags to the market. I wondered if I was the only person to notice the accumulating and, in my opinion, unacceptable single-use plastic bag trash. I shared the problem I had with plastic bag pollution and suggested a solution.

I set off with the few samples I had and began knocking on doors, talking to shop owners on Columbus Avenue. I began with a few traditional, expandable "filet"-style string bags like I'd used in Europe years earlier. (I had noticed that when I used these bags in my neighborhood, I got curious glances, occasional questions, and a few "Where can I get one of those?") When a few shop owners responded with small orders, it was time to take the next tiny steps: I needed product—and a business name.

Own It by Naming It

Back to the kitchen table, where all great things happen . . .

While eating dinner one evening—with my infant son in my arms—I asked my husband, Blake, what we should call this fledgling business. Without missing a beat (he's a songwriter), he said "Eco-Bags." That was the whole discussion. Eco-Bags Products was born.

Side note: It was the first time the prefix "eco" had ever been followed by "bags." Had we known then what we know now about branding, using or not using descriptive words, and online search, our simple approach may not have worked. But at least we knew enough to protect our newly born tiny brand with trademark registrations. My advice? Find an intellectual property (IP) trademark lawyer to help you get started. It will cost you less to do it right the first time. Don't do it yourself. Trust me.

Need to Do vs. Nice to Do

With any new startup, there's a lot of juggling involved, which can create stress. It feels like there's never enough time. The next not-so-tiny but important steps in setting up my business included:

- ◆ Talking with (and then retaining) a lawyer
- ◆ Getting an accountant
- ◆ Choosing the legal structure (we chose an S corp)
- ◆ Finding a manufacturer
- ◆ Ordering product

Oh yeah—we needed to find more customers too.

The flurry of work landed on my desk and I was soon overwhelmed. The urgency to take care of everything quickly was layered on top of our growing financial and family demands. That's when I became aware of how important it is to prioritize tasks and separate "need to do" from "nice to do."

Having your own business, especially in the beginning, can certainly be overwhelming—if you let it. But that's not the Tiny Business way.

Every day I reviewed my priorities, taking care of "need to do" first and putting "nice to do" to the side. Sure, it got uncomfortable when the "nice to do" pile got so big it began to block the "need to do" pile just by volume.

Need to do, nice to do.

"
You can complete those "nice to do's" or you can throw them out. If something's important, rest assured, it will reappear.
"

Most of us share a tendency to want to please and to say yes more than we say no. We're afraid we may miss some big opportunity or insight if we don't respond to everything that comes our way. Those unanswered emails lurk in our in-box, distracting us from our real priorities. We must handle them one way or another—answer them or get them out of our sight—before they wreak havoc on our focus. We need to stay intentional and focused on our priorities (consciously chosen limitations, remember?).

When you set out in a direction, with purpose and intention, opportunities tend to arise that are in sync with what you're doing. Like magic.

Just Fine vs. Perfect

To find a manufacturer, I naïvely faxed every consulate in Europe I could think of, who kindly passed my inquiry along to the right people. The Germans responded almost immediately with pricing and samples. The Spanish responded a few months later, the Italians about two years later, and we never got a response from the French. The German product was like the French one that had inspired me, but with less style. It was good enough to get started. I ordered a small amount of inventory and turned my hallway into a storage and distribution center.

66

Good enough is a great start.

99

Now that I had enough product to fill the few small orders from local shop owners, my ears were on the ground listening to what could be next. I don't remember how we found out about Earth Day, but we did. The second Earth

Day in 1990 (the original event took place in 1970) was going to be a huge street fair and celebration along Sixth Avenue in midtown. It wasn't a stretch to see that we needed to be there. All I needed to do was send in an application, get a vendor permit, and pay a small fee.

I decided that Earth Day would serve as the real test to premier our ECOBAGS brand: a table filled with reusable bags for sale at an event dedicated to saving the earth from pollution. We air-freighted an order from overseas, guessing on quantity. We were cautious—we knew we couldn't eat bags if Earth Day was a bomb for any reason—but optimistic. We took that proverbial (but manageable) leap of faith.

Within four hours we were sold out and had collected thousands of dollars in cash. My husband, my parents, and I were all behind the table talking about what inspired us to start this venture, selling product hand over fist! The Earth Day event revealed the nerve we wanted to tap into.

The Earth Day success garnered us a mention in a sizeable article in *Newsday*. We got our first taste of media exposure and mail orders began flooding in. (It was 1990, remember?) Luckily, we had a hallway long enough to warehouse and distribute orders from. The business was our new roommate!

Our shipping service, the US Post Office, was a few blocks away. The postal workers would only sell lick-on stamps and the lines wrapped around the block. Imagine waiting an hour to get stamps for a hundred packages with an infant in a stroller and then having to lick and stick stamps onto each package. There was no glamour in this reality, and I began to question everything. Fortunately, I had a partner in crime.

Share Your Story—Everywhere with Everyone!

Shopping at our local natural products store one day, my husband struck up a conversation with a guy unloading product from his truck for the store. Blake pitched him our business and the driver shared our story with the folks back at headquarters. It turned out the driver worked with Stow Mills, the largest natural products distributor on the East Coast at the time (they later became part of United Natural Foods, Inc.). And they were interested in us! Within a couple months we had ten times the number of orders. We had hit pay dirt! We had found our niche, supplying the growing natural products industry through distribution.

We continued to sell directly to consumers, but we decided to focus on our wholesale volume business because it was in keeping with our Tiny Business value of time for family. With a wholesale business, office hours could be flexibly managed during a typical nine-to-five workday. We consciously limited our consumer business, which freed us up to build relationships with buyers for repeatable orders.[1]

Exercise: Practice Takes Practice

Change is hard when you try to do too much. Instead, do smaller bits. Here's a little exercise to get you in the practice. Watch how your tiny steps add up to change your brain, change the way you think, and change the way you are in the world. Try it.

Set a timer for twenty minutes every day for thirty days. Choose an activity you don't normally do to focus on intently for those twenty minutes—for example, write haikus, play an instrument, make something out of clay, draw, or meditate. Start at the same time and end when the timer goes off regardless of where you are in the process. Note how your understanding of the activity shifts over those thirty days and how you can apply those insights to other parts of your life.

Tiny Business 80/20 Rule

Moving quickly from the dream stage to the reality of building a business was, to be honest, exciting, disruptive, and challenging. My goals of making a living and doing something that matters were being met. However, my third and driving intention—to make work work for me versus being consumed by it—was not happening naturally. I had to figure out how to manage my time before it started managing me.

One approach was putting start and stop times on my daily schedule and moving forward with "just fine" and "good enough." If I allowed an hour to do tasks in the morning, for example, I would start at 10:00 a.m. and end at 11:00 a.m., moving whatever wasn't completed to the next day. I was able to chip away at things with consistent attention. It was the beginning of learning when and what to let go of. For that I made up an 80/20 rule and thought I was being original . . . but I was not.

The Pareto principle states that 80 percent of results are produced from 20 percent of efforts. It's an accepted principle in business. In Tiny Business, 80/20 has another layer. Consider that for every 80 percent of results, we need to give ourselves a minimum of 20 percent permission to trip, stumble, or fail and reboot. Daily priorities are a moving target. Your core—what you stand for—will get challenged, too, but it shouldn't change daily.

Soften Your Focus 20 Percent of the Time

The exercise of setting up rules and then having to break them—which we know always happens—leads to a sense of failure, a feeling that you're not good enough. The original intention gets lost in mind crap.

By setting up the 80/20 rule, you give yourself permission to break the rules for whatever comes up 20 percent of the time. The point is we can't control everything, and being perfect isn't a good strategy.

66

Nothing is risk-free . . .

99

Instead of going for 100 percent, focus and be on task 80 percent of the time and allow 20 percent for a softer focus. That way you won't waste time being mad at yourself and thinking you're a failure.

A softer focus is what you have when you are not going for immediate fixes. It's when you breathe, step away, and create the room to gain new insights. It's when you get a glass of water (more on that next). It provides the space to let your mind make connections on its own.

Do the best you can and work with that. Not everyone will agree with me. But, hey, do they have weekends off?

Get a Glass of Water

When my children would scrape a knee, fall off a bicycle, or come screaming into the house because whatever disaster had just happened, I immediately gave them a glass of water to drink. The action of taking a glass from the shelf, filling it with water, and having them drink the water before I asked what happened opened the space for a little more calm and focus. The same tactic works well for business. Most business emergencies are not life threatening, so taking a minute to refocus is a very good thing.

When confronted with situations that demand your immediate attention—it might be a customer, an employee, or a cash problem—you have to determine whether it is an emergency. Do I need to stop what I'm doing to address the situation? If I don't, will everything fall apart? Can I put it in the "parking lot" and address it later?

You'd be surprised what can happen when a business finds itself in a tight spot. For example, if the organic shampoo you make has a formula that uses a specific ingredient that suddenly becomes unavailable and a similar nonorganic ingredient is available at a lower cost and you have orders pending, what do you do? If the promise to your employees is a four-day holiday weekend and a rush job comes that will pay handsomely but will impact that promise, what do you do? These challenges can only be solved by regularly returning to your stated Tiny Business values in order to make decisions that are in alignment with them.

I had started out wanting a set of conflicting priorities: time with my new family while building a business that would give me that time. I didn't know yet how much skill I would need to manage the business to get the results I wanted. I didn't fully understand the force of a new venture or the energy it takes to guide and ride it. It takes a real commitment to be disciplined and requires ease in situations that aren't easy.

In business you need to be able to pivot quickly. Agility matters. If an opportunity comes your way, your ability to respond quickly is important. For that to happen, you need to practice seeing all your options through the lens of "why."

Don't Let Business Become Busy-ness

I have to admit that sometimes I was an alarmist, sending my team in all directions to fix things immediately when many of them didn't share my sense of urgency. What I needed to do was step back to look at what was happening through the lens of my Tiny Business priorities. Business, after all, can become just busy-ness. If you rush to fix a problem, it may not be the best fix and you may miss a golden opportunity.

Instead, my advice is to take the time to apply thought and intention to the problem. What you want is to be able to assess and respond, not react and regret your decisions. Before you even start, consider the language you're using. If you replace "problem" or "challenge" with "opportunity," the window will automatically open wider for insights.

Here's my Tiny Business system for reviewing problems (also known as opportunities) as they arise.

1. Go get a glass of water.

2. Reframe the problem as an opportunity.

3. Figure out which bucket it falls into. All "opportunities" fall into one of three buckets. Here's how to process each:

    a. I've seen this before. I know what I can do. I have options and they are X, Y, and Z.

    b. I've seen some of this before but not all. Here's a list of what's the same and what's different. I may need help with this.

    c. I'm completely blindsided. I don't even know who to call first: my accountant, lawyer, coach, or associate. I need to take this apart and see if anything is recognizable. Let me just start calling to figure this out. A conversation might spark an insight.

4. Act according to your Tiny Business priorities, even if it means losing the immediate business. Make the space for possible alternative approaches that align with your priorities.

"

Don't go mental, go incremental.

"

The big wisdom I'm offering here is to get a glass of water and take a moment to refocus on your priorities before you jump in. Break it down before you break down!

Chapter Four

Listen to Your Tiny Voice

❝
I can't say I was a perfect Tiny Business entrepreneur when I started.
❞

I can say, however, that I grew more focused with practice over time and that the advice I'm sharing will save you time and money.

When you start a business, you are journeying into a marketplace. You need to listen to your "why" to choose your path. What I had from the very beginning was a deep connection to why I was doing what I was doing. And as an actor, I was trained to listen.

> *Listen to listen*
> *Compassion and empathy*
> *What's needed will be*
> —Tiny Business haiku

After two years, ECOBAGS were still being met with curiosity. Our product and concept were still relatively new, and they were sparking conversations. We were embraced by a small group of people who shared our passion of "cleaning up the planet one bag at a time." They wanted to share our concept too! That's when I learned the value of having a good story and listening to where and how it lands.

66

A good story is an invitation to connect.

99

For us, it was an opening for like-minded people to come together and participate in the co-creation of a brand and a movement. We were tiny but we were powerful.

What I learned is that the product is not the thing; it's the platform, the messenger.

The story—that's the thing.

The early adopters shared and embraced our story as their own, and they took it further than we ever could have. They told us we were more than a practical product—we were an aspirational brand. We used a lifestyle accessory to spark a conversation that inspired and empowered a cultural shift. We did this by listening to our tiny voice that was filled with passion for our "why" and to our customers experiencing the power of our "why" through our products.

You have a good story. Tell it. And listen to how people respond to it.

Exercise: Get Clear On Your Story with OPM

You know your brand better than anyone, but you may not be the best at communicating it or have the budget to hire a marketing team. Here's an exercise to open your thinking that won't drain you. OPM is an acronym for "other people's money" but in this exercise, it means "other people's marketing."

Think of this exercise as a shortcut that's a lot like those *Mad Libs* books where you fill in the blanks to create your own twist on an existing story. Find brands you love and study their marketing and advertising. Pull ads out of magazines or off the web—wherever you find something that speaks to you. Try on the campaigns of larger, more well-established brands. Analyze their stories, how they tell them, who they tell them to, and how they position themselves. Put your brand—your images and copy—into their marketing pieces. First go with their perspectives, then make up your own. Guaranteed, you will find new insights and approaches.

The point isn't to copy someone else's work outright; it's to leverage skillfully created platforms that inspire you. It's an easy way to spark ideas. Sometimes my idea will end up being the opposite of the brand I studied; sometimes it will be very close. The point is to absorb what is pertinent and bounce off what isn't.

This is also an awesome exercise for your own personal branding—who you are as a leader of your business. Research business leader profile pieces in magazines. See what is being said about a leader you admire. Then think about what could be said about you. What can you say about yourself? Remember, this is not about boasting but about building up your communication tool kit so that you have it at your fingertips.

With a Tiny Business, the mindset is to grow sustainably, staying focused on the reason you started in the first place, practicing patience, and being consistent and persistent with what you stand for. It's about how to get the most with "whatcha got" while staying true to "who you are." This is expansion through mindful marketing, listening, and making intentional connections.

Mindful Marketing

Chaos can reign with marketing. You need to decide where to put your best efforts for best results, and you need to be able to measure those results. You can't do everything.

What distinguishes you as a Tiny Business is your articulated intentions, your journey, and how telling your story inspires others. Focusing on what value you can bring to others sends out an invitation to engage. Here are two low-cost, accessible ways to market your "why":

1. Win an award.
2. Get media/influencer attention.

Awards are Low-Hanging Fruit

I've found the return on awards to be very high even without a win. It's all about raising your profile and building momentum. The more you get, the more you're seen; the more you're seen, the more you get.

Find awards that are relevant. Look for ones that will give you a good return on investment, the kind of exposure you want in return for your efforts. A good place to start is your local business chamber or business media outlets. They both use awards ceremonies to gather the business community around them and promote themselves.

It's a win-win scenario: you want to be seen and they want to be seen.

My marketing director (my sister) submitted me for the Westchester Business Council Entrepreneur of the Year award and I won! I also nominated myself for a women in business diversity award with a local news publication. A month later I received a call saying I was nominated in two categories. At first I was flattered until I remembered I'd nominated myself. LOL!

The exposure was great. Every nominee was featured in the news publication with full bios and a short essay on diversity. The publication went out to thousands of subscribers. The request to vote went out in at least three more issues, each time with a picture of everyone nominated (more press!). Plus I leveraged the coverage by sharing it with my business associates. They didn't know I'd nominated myself.

I did not get the big award but, along with all other nominees, I was invited to come to the ceremony to receive recognition. I walked into the reception and saw people I knew, who introduced me to their people. For a simple submission that took me three hours, I got more than ten touchpoints[1] in the media and in person:

- ◆ 6 placements in business media (before and after)
- ◆ 1 placement in event program
- ◆ 1 peer recognition at event
- ◆ 1 peer connection at event
- ◆ 2 event group photos with name tag

- 1 blog post
- 1 social media post
- 2 relationship interactions with potential for business

It was a very efficient way to get exposure.

Getting Press Is Easier Than You Think

As a Tiny Business, you have carefully articulated your "why"—the things that matter to you, your business, and the world—and woven them into your brand story. You have something of value. You have exactly what media needs: a story with a perspective and a takeaway.

Media placements don't always tie back immediately to transactional business, but they do build your profile as a thought leader, which leads to more and stronger relationships, which then lead to more opportunities.

But media placement cannot just be about you and your story. Ultimately, it's about you adding value to the outlet and their audience. For this reason, it is essential that you carefully research the outlets that are the right fit for you. This is not about throwing spaghetti against the wall to see what sticks. It's about using your Tiny laser focus to connect with like-minded communities and share the value you are creating.

I was recently contacted by a writer for a story in *Inc.* magazine. The writer knew from a *Time* feature she'd done on my business seven years ago that I would be a good source to quote. We'd stayed in touch over the years. The writer initially found me because our brand was featured on a major TV show (more on that in the next chapter). This is just one connection that has played out over a decade. There have been many more.

On a practical note, make and keep your marketing brand assets (everything about you and your business) organized and ready for use. Below is a starter list of things you want to have ready. Have all assets in editable form or in multiple forms so that you can easily customize or send assets out with a cover letter.

Brand Assets to Always Have On Hand

- Your complete LinkedIn profile
- Two-sentence summary describing yourself and your company
- Short bio: 125–150 words
- Long bio: 300 words
- Professional headshot in high- and low-res formats
- Alternative images that can be released to PR and media in high- and low-res formats
- All social media handles and website
- Complete list of your and your company's awards and recognitions
- Brand guidelines

Give to Get (Visibility)

I've been invited to donate product and time to organizations of all sizes. When you donate as an individual to an organization, it's because it makes you feel good. When you give as a Tiny Business, you feel good *and* it provides multiple ways to create mutually beneficial relationships.

One thing is true of most organizations: they are hungry for funding, and they are happy to receive whatever they can for free. What they offer is visibility to their supporters. But for this to work for your Tiny Business, you have to place a real monetary value on what you're giving. Negotiate a trade for visibility versus just giving it away.

When considering a donation or sponsorship:

- ◆ Put a market value on your goods or services.
- ◆ Negotiate on a full or partial value exchange (e.g., tickets to the event, advertisement in the program, use of their email marketing list, etc.).
- ◆ Get a donation letter for the IRS with value stated.
- ◆ Ensure visibility:
  - ▸ Web links and logos on the event website
  - ▸ Logo and write-up in the program
  - ▸ Shout-out at the event
  - ▸ Logo placement on promotional items
  - ▸ Brand literature to be given out with promotional items
  - ▸ Social media mentions (by you and the organization you are donating to)
- ◆ Approve all text and brand/logo use before it goes to print.

- Get sample assets (e.g., programs and other places your brand appears) for your files.

Listen to Connect

Let's talk about connections a bit more.

As a new business owner, you've just joined an ecosystem. You now have relationships with customers, suppliers, and possibly subcontractors such as tech support, graphic design, legal, and accounting. If you don't need money-access relationships (e.g., loans and credit lines) yet, you will soon. And here's the thing about everyone you're working with:

❝

You need them and they need you to do business.

❞

It's not always a level playing field—who needs who more—but it is an interconnected system of goods and services.

With Eco-Bags Products, we knew we were onto an opportunity for a powerful brand and growth, even though we were still tiny. With limited resources and a young family at home, the next step was to figure out how to connect to more of our tribe with efficiency and speed.

"

We needed to make our mark.

"

First, I asked a friend to move us from a "word-only" trademark to a logo design. Then we added the new design to permanent cloth labels to brand each and every bag. That single decision has been an incredible multiplier— our simplest, most effective marketing to date. That little stitched logo carries our story all over the world, connecting us with new and repeat customers. That tiny tag has big meaning.

Evolution of a brand logo

Think Differently

When we launched ECOBAGS, we gained traction right away. Sales took off immediately. But the larger market-place for our goods was still very sleepy (read: low sales volume), and we knew how big the potential for growth was. Initial sales had been "attraction" sales, as in "build it and they will come," but we were moving past that honey-moon stage. Now I had to go out and find more buyers, make more connections, and connect more dots. Not familiar with "push" sales and with no desire to do business that way, I was lost.

On the marketing side, I had a compelling story and the love of early adopters. On the operational side, I had beautifully designed and made goods. But the cash register needed to ring much more often. It was time for this Tiny Business to pick up the pace and gain momentum.

The scope of what needed to happen was overwhelming. I was tested to the point where I quit the business a few times and even took a part-time job . . . briefly. I quit that too! Refreshed after my mini break, I continued. Nothing happens fast, anyway.

66

It takes time to create value.

99

"Every transition which I've sought in life has taken me eighteen months with clear focus to get going."

—Drew Lehman, Environmental and
Workplace Entrepreneur

Instead of going wide into the unknown, I chose to go deep into the somewhat known. I went in the direction of where our brand was already getting love. I picked the natural products trade shows since I already had entrée through our distributor.

How do you measure the return on investment when you don't know the potential range of return? I had to go back to a few rules I'd set up. I took time to break down the trade show opportunity into small bits and pieces. I made an honest review of all my resources, funds, and inventory. And as I was about to release the check, I had an idea for how to keep the cash, expand my brand, and pay for our booth space in one fell swoop.

I contacted the show office, offering to barter custom-printed bags at full price as show promo marketing in exchange for booth space. It was a new idea then; now, it's an established income stream. They said yes, so I set out for my first trade show.

66

As a Tiny Business in start-up mode or in full swing, never underestimate the value of seeking out or asking for visibility.

99

Think differently.

Most conferences will have sponsorship levels that you can purchase or trade for with in-kind goods. Again, work with your full market value to bring the best value to your business. And you can definitely trade for the value of the conference registration. There's a huge savings there with an upside in visibility.

Trade shows and industry conferences aren't just about selling to one kind of buyer; they are about joining a community at an event that, over years, can become like a family reunion. We quickly saw potential business with retailers and marketers. We also saw how both of those types of relationships were touchpoints to hundreds, possibly thousands more.

Touchpoints can be points of distribution, goods or ideas, companies, or influencers. Every touchpoint matters. And just like our product with our tiny tag was a touchpoint to our brand, each person we established a dialogue with was a touchpoint to their community.

66

We are communities of people,
not just consumers.

99

Trade shows and conferences are where you go to listen and learn as well as be heard. They are where the connectivity of business happens, where you go to expand relationships. The word "networking" has always held a negative, forced connotation for me. By shifting my focus to listening and learning, I was able to more holistically expand my network.

It's also important to state that sometimes there's no place like home for building relationships, creating fans, and spreading influence. For years I looked outside my circles to find influencers until I woke up to see that friends and friends of friends were whom I needed to spend time with. The more touchpoints you make, the wider your ideas can spread to attract business.

Listening to the Naysayers

Not everyone we connected with became an immediate member of our tribe. You can treat the naysayers as background noise, but if you do you may miss insights that will give you a competitive edge. Remember, they are part of the business ecosystem too. You may not be ready for them, or they for you, but trends change.

What worked for building our Tiny Business was to listen closely to our own fan base and be informed but not distracted by our naysayers—all while the competition was growing. A cacophonous movement was being built (the green movement) and we were, literally, an accessory to it.

By engaging with and listening to the naysayers, I learned that it's not always about the brand or the idea; it's also about how easily we can fit into a category and be set up for success. For example, I was set up for independent buyers. The naysayers introduced me to the more complex broker-rep-distributor world of commissions and discounts for growth.

For the folks who walked past me with blank stares because my brand was of no value to them: what I had didn't fit with what they needed or how they worked at that moment. My job was not to sell to them. They would cost too much in time and energy.

My job was to talk to them, to get them to tell me more about what they needed and why, and who else they knew. I figured they would come around at some point; I just didn't bank on it. And even if they never came around and we just went out for a beer, I knew we had a connection that would play out in some way some day.

Trusting Your Voice Takes Practice

With a Tiny Business, you practice trust by making decisions rooted in your intentions over and over again.

When opportunity knocks, you decide to open the door wide, slightly, or not at all. Like a bonsai tree that's pruned regularly to determine how big it gets and what shape it takes, you are selective about what work you want and don't want, need and don't need.

When you are listening to your Tiny voice and allowing it to speak for you, you are taking care of you—first and foremost—so that you can take care of your business. Trust that the energy and excitement you are creating will be felt and shared.

You can't stand for everything.

Part III

Practice Your "How"

Over and Over and Over Again . . .

Chapter Five

Be Ready for Takeoff

"
I didn't watch The Oprah Winfrey Show.
"

In the mid-2000s, Oprah was the number one afternoon talk show host on one of the most famous television shows in the United States (and possibly the world), but she just wasn't on my radar. I became aware, however, that there were lots of women who stopped everything to watch her; among them was my close friend and neighbor, April, and my mother-in-law, Ales. Almost every day my neighbor would relay stories from the show to me.

I can actually pinpoint when it occurred to me that my brand ECOBAGS had to be featured on *Oprah*. It was 2006. Al Gore was talking about climate change on the national stage; hormone-free milk, Whole Foods Market, and organic everything were getting ink; and my pioneering concept of reusable bags was being warmly adopted by the fringe. I was confident Oprah was my ticket to the mainstream with her huge, devoted audience who listened to her like a god.

I knew getting to Oprah wouldn't be easy, but because I hadn't put her on a pedestal I figured the distance between us could be conquered. All I needed to do was find the right person. That was when I first understood the power of tapping the relationships I'd been building.

For the first time in fifteen years, I reached out to someone in public relations. I had always done everything on my own—I got onto QVC and the pages of the *New York Post* and more by myself. I thought buying publicity was too expensive. I was independent and scrappy . . . until now. Now, I needed a connection to Oprah.

I only knew one person who did PR: Nancy Shenker from a local firm, the On-Switch Agency. And I only knew her because I'd sat next to her at a local meeting for women in business and had her card on my desk. I called Nancy, reintroduced myself, and said I wanted my brand to be on Oprah. This was not a quantitative, budgeted, or studied approach. It was a gut move.

To Nancy's credit, she didn't laugh. She didn't dissuade me. She did say it was a long shot but that she would do her best. And so I signed on. I accepted her terms and fee of $4,000 a month for a run of four months and began meeting with her team.

Keep in mind that $16,000 was a leap of faith for a Tiny Business with just $700,000 in gross revenue. I probably financed it with one of my many 0 percent cash-advance credit cards.

Furthermore, four months was a very tight timeline. But it was a risk I was willing to take. It was January 2007 and I knew that in April, Oprah would be doing her very first Earth Day show to coincide with the annual Earth Day event (the same one we launched at seventeen years before!). And so April became our target month.

The Oprah Effect

Nancy activated her network, finding publicist Ann-Marie Nieves, who had a line into someone on the show and who "got" what we were about. We prepped and waited in ready position. Our narrative was in place and we had a warehouse full of bags, but there were only two of us in the office, one phone line, a fax line, and our brand new, just integrated, scalable cloud platform. We were as ready as we could be—but still not knowing how ready we needed to be.

We got a "maybe" in early April. Then the show producers called to request samples only seventy-two hours before the show was going live. We used the fastest UPS service to ship our product out and continued to wait. Being invited to send product still wasn't confirmation we'd make it onto the show, but we were getting closer. Then we got the "yes" call. ECOBAGS would be on the show in less than thirty hours visible to an audience of millions!

My mom came to my house, as did my Oprah-watching neighbor. I cannot remember if my husband was in the room. He was probably at work. We turned on the TV and I saw my brand on national TV on *The Oprah Winfrey*

Show. Oprah and her guest, TreeHugger's Simran Sethi, talked about ways to "go green" while pointing to our reusable bags as one impactful action to take.

In those few seconds, Oprah changed the trajectory of my business, the green products category, and millions of viewers' opinion of what can be done to clean up the planet. She sent this Tiny Business on a wild ride into the unknown. We experienced the "Oprah effect" firsthand.

But Be Careful What You Ask for . . .

The phones started ringing off the hook with people saying, "I want to go green." Orders came in practically non-stop for months and then with a repeat of the same show a year later, orders flooded in again. Our integrated, scalable, cloud-based system held up, thankfully, but we had to get a bigger office and add phone lines and staff immediately.

We went from $700,000 to $2.2 million in a year and from a two-person office to five and growing. We had back orders for up to three months. We were overwhelmed, but we patiently communicated to all our new customers, setting expectations on delivery and welcoming them into our eco-friendly world like they were dinner guests. Throughout the insanity of the pre- and post-Oprah months, we maintained regular business hours and I managed to swim daily. My personal take on this was, "We're not running blood. There are no bag emergencies."

In addition to increasing sales, we were now catapulted from our tiny niche into a wildly popular category of green products. Oprah gave millions of people a touchpoint, inspiring them to think about our environment as something to respect and protect. Big ideas were communicated because she pointed to our brand! And we went from being a fledging to a fast-growth business overnight.

❝

But businesspeople were also watching.

❞

They always are. They watch smaller companies grow ideas and then jump in with well-financed production and branding to meet the mainstream demand, capitalizing on ideas as quickly as they can. Not only that, there were signs we would be entering an economic downturn and a recession was looming.

❝

Stress is when you don't know what you don't know but you know you need to know more.

❞

It no longer mattered that we were there first, the pioneers of a new concept. We had to move fast. I had to figure out how to manage rapid growth fast. That's when the real stress kicked in. I didn't know what I didn't know—but needed to know—about growing and building a bigger business. In the next sections, I'll tell you all that I learned so that you can be better prepared than I was when your business takes off.

Anticipating Growth AND Slowdowns

With the Oprah lift, our Tiny Business needed more resources. Our pre-Oprah existence was a small home office with a constellation of freelancers and vendors. That's how we kept overhead down and cash easily flowing. Post-Oprah, we needed to expand rapidly. Confident, we moved to a large and then larger, more expensive office downtown, adding Andrew Dyer as our VP of Operations and staff. Our overhead costs went from low to high. Even with all this expansion going on, we managed to stay true to our tiny core; we didn't waiver personally or professionally.

We committed to maintaining regular work hours (no working weekends—not even email!) and did not succumb to pressure to compete with lower-cost and less eco-friendly options. We knew that would be a race to the bottom and our brand would suffer. From a very practical business perspective, competing with lower-cost options, while potentially profitable in the short term, would have added operational and financial challenges.

But here is where we went wrong: we were moving fast, restructuring the business based on the new current demand with future growth in mind. All we could see ahead was growth. We were not being conservative with our spending, and we were not yet working with forecasts or budgets. We weren't wasting money, but we weren't saving it either. We'd grown slowly for years, then had explosive 3x growth in just a few months.

Then came the Great Recession. We didn't think we'd be in the firing line so soon, and we weren't prepared for it.

Unlike many others, we managed to survive the recession—but we didn't come out unscathed. It was quite a ride! So what did we learn?

"

In business, you are not alone. You are part of an ecosystem and you do not have the luxury of avoidance.

"

You may be involved in your own reality, but yours is not the only real one. Listen to the news, family, and friends, even if you're busy and you think what's going on "out there" doesn't apply to you. Prepare for *all* the "what-ifs."

And if you take even some of the following advice, you will be more prepared than we were.

"The water has receded hundreds of feet further than normal for a low tide. Do you want to go look at seashells?"

How to Be Ready for Anything

- ♦ Keep your overhead low.

- ♦ Expand with caution (don't rent that big office until you're bursting at the seams).

- ♦ Know your lending sources before you need them.

- ♦ Lead with agility.

- ♦ Practice pivoting (keep on asking yourself "what if?" from many perspectives).

- ♦ Always be forecasting (more on this in the next chapter).

Pay Attention to Take Action

Once the economy began to take a downturn, everyone was running scared. The Great Recession hadn't happened yet, but it was about to happen and it was going to be really big. Businesses were cutting back on staff just in case. Others were reducing inventory. Meanwhile, I'd just hired a whole office and was on a growth ride with zero experience reducing anything.

At Eco-Bags Products, we were humming along, riding the Oprah wave. Orders were flowing. Cash was good. In hindsight, we should've pulled back and saved for just in case. A classic business mistake. We got caught up in our own reality. I thought we were impervious, that whatever was about to happen wouldn't take a bite out of us. I was listening, but I wasn't paying attention and I wasn't taking any actions.

Instead of creating forecasts to project our cash needs and cutting back staff hours, I signed up everyone in the office for weekly yoga. I approached what I thought was just "financial hysteria" with mindfulness and stretching. It's what I thought we needed to survive. We were still doing great. Our sales were strong. I was even entertaining the idea of expanding amidst the ensuing chaos with a group of interested partners. I ignored my gut instincts to cut back and save. It all felt just too hard, way outside my comfort zone, so I avoided dealing with it.

66

If you love stress, practice avoidance.

99

Get Help

In the span of a year, I watched the business sputter to half its gross revenue. We were still way above sales prior to the Oprah spurt, but we were now dipping below our comfort zone. We started devouring cash because we hadn't reduced our expenses quickly enough. We were in a downward spiral. Goodbye profit, hello hole. We didn't have a cash reserve to rely on or financial resources to tap. The sky was getting dark.

I went off on vacation, leaving my struggling company to fend for itself with an outward appearance of *joie de vivre*. I was working under my "vacations first" Tiny Business priority. Anyone who knew me, however, could see I was preoccupied.

I was at dance camp, supposedly focusing on my creativity and connecting with nature and movement, but I couldn't really focus. I took action in the form of an "illegal" cell call from my platform tent in the middle of the Connecticut woods to get help from a friend's CFO. She advised me on what I needed to do.

The strategy wasn't rocket science. I needed to muster my courage and take a few logical and doable actions. Calmed, I finished the vacation (what's another three days away from the office?) and then began getting my business in order. Here's what I did:

How to Prepare for a Downturn

- ✦ Expand cash flow.
- ✦ Slow down accounts payable.
- ✦ Negotiate extended terms with suppliers by communicating what's going on.
- ✦ Speed up accounts receivable by taking credit card payments, offering early payment discounts, or other incentives.
- ✦ Trim staff hours.
- ✦ Focus on need to have versus nice to have (i.e., profitable revenue-driving projects only).
- ✦ Share what's going on with the team. Get buy-in. They may have great ideas to add.

I was overwhelmed. Fortunately, a very capable and likeable CEO, Alan Shapiro, was referred to me. Without taking time to carefully interview anyone else, I offered him a job—the job was to take my pain away and put the company back together.

I reduced my compensation to nothing to be able to pay him, and he went to work to do all the things I didn't feel confident doing. He did great. He had been a CEO of a larger company and knew better than me how to engage, lead, and direct my team.

Outsourcing my stress allowed me time to regroup, keep my free time prioritized, and see what the business needed next. I consciously limited my role in my own business in order to stay true to my Tiny Business principles, which, let's not forget, included remaining a profitable company. It wasn't easy letting go of the reins, but it's exactly what needed to happen.

Stay *Connected*

Remember the Erector sets we played with as kids? All the pieces connect to form a whole. That's how we are as a business community. If you need a nature image, we're a huge lily pad with our roots all growing together in the muck and tangled up. We need each other to survive.

"

Everyone's a touchpoint, someone who may be in a position to offer help when you need it.

"

Before we needed cash support and before the recession hit, my accountant, Michael, did a really great thing. He introduced me to his contact at the bank, Josephine.

He knew what I didn't know yet: getting access to money is easier if you have a good credit score and an established relationship with a banker.

The CEO I hired to get us out of our GRH (Great Recession hole) was referred to me by someone I'd had coffee with who was referred to me for a reason I cannot even remember. When you talk to people about who you are and what you want to do and how you want to grow, sometimes they listen.

> **“**
>
> ## When you build business relationships, you are building your fan base too.
>
> **”**

A long time ago, my first and only customs broker for decades, Guido Zhender,[1] gave great advice:

> *"If you get into trouble or need something, don't go silent or drop out. The best thing you can do is pick up the phone, stay connected, work out a solution together. Talk to your suppliers. Work out terms. It will make your relationship stronger."*

And that's what we did. While we were struggling to adjust our business during the recession, so were our partners, suppliers, and customers. Instead of avoiding our commitments, we called everyone and let them know what was going on. We prepared for the harder conversations, having notes on financials to reference if needed. We did not hide from what needed to be done. We renegotiated terms, paying late when we needed, and speeding up payments when we could.

When the Competition Gets Tough, Collaborate

After Oprah and all the resulting media exposure, our reusable bag concept was out of the stable. Even during the recession, companies were smelling profit and stepping in to crowd our space. At the same time, other entrepreneurs were having their own aha moments, starting out as humbly as we did, to address the same urgent problem.

It didn't take too long before there were multiple brands like ours on the market, brands that took the problem seriously and were addressing it with gusto and integrity. Here's one thing we did right: we saw these other brands as competition, sure, but we also saw them as possible collaborators to address the bigger problem—plastic pollution. So instead of putting our resources into competing with these brands, we looked at it differently.

We asked ourselves, what if they sell and promote our brand and we do the same for theirs? What if we talk about them in our marketing channels and share their stories? What if we take a cooperative, generous stance and ask the same of them? What if we practiced co-opetition?

Co-opetition = Competition + Cooperation
—Onyeka Obiocha, Director of Innovation,
Yale University, Center for Public Service
and Social Justice

You don't want to be the only brand in a category—not in the long run. Early brands have to first identify a market and open it up. But once they do, there is room for other brands. I've always thought the more the merrier. We were the first in our category, and it was not only a little lonely but challenging to find buyers willing to open shelf space for us. Not only was there no track record on our brand, there was no track record for our product category.

If there's only one brand of something on a shelf or in a search, there's nothing to compare. And, ultimately, customers want options, to be able to choose which brand they want. It's a losing proposition to try to own a whole category. The better focus for your time and energy is to go deep on the value you bring. What better way to bring attention to that value than by collaborating with other like-minded brands?

Co-opetition

Onyeka Obiocha, now director of innovation at Yale University's Center for Public Service and Social Justice, coined the term "co-opetition," a combination of cooperation and competition. It's how to leverage partnerships to promote growth, he explains. This is what we were doing over fifteen years ago before it had a name!

Working with ChicoBag, a similar brand with the same mission, co-opetition was an easy decision. ChicoBag's bag style was very different than ours, and they were manufacturing in China. We were already fifteen years

"We have to come downtown more often!"

into a very solid relationship with our partners in India. To design bags like theirs (even with prototypes we'd developed years earlier) would have put a financial burden on us and strained existing relationships. We decided early on to sell their products to our customers and they, a few years later, added ours to their mix.

Our decisions made it easy for customers to shop with us for all their reusable bag needs. We were able to profitably sell their brand, capitalize on their marketing, and satisfy our customers with one action. This wasn't a blind exchange, however. We went into the relationship with our eyes wide open, discussing and agreeing to our relationship terms.

❝
Do you want to spend your time creating fans or fending off foes?
❞

If your business hits a nerve, generates a buzz, and looks doable, then others will want to be like you and do like you with the same kind of values and focus. There's no reason any single business needs to own the entire town. A town with one restaurant only draws a certain number of people. When you add another restaurant and a coffee shop, you add options. More people come, more people choose, more businesses open and thrive. It's the law of momentum.

Cooperative Marketing

Another option to amplify your reach is through cooperative marketing: finding brands that are simpatico with your own and who are playing in the same sandbox but are not in direct competition with the same product. Call them out, celebrate their stories, and co-market.

When Sandra Harris of ECOlunchbox launched her brand, she called me out of the blue and asked if I would be her mentor. She'd seen what I did with Eco-Bags Products and she wanted to be a Tiny Business too. She was like me when I started: a mom with a product to fix a problem (replace plastic lunch containers with 100 percent plastic-free reusable eco-friendly lunchware) who wanted to make a nice income.

> *"I learn by connecting with others willing to share their experience. Sure, there are fiercely competitive and suspicious people guarding their secret sauce, but they generally don't have the big ideas. I've found generosity breeds generosity and spreads big ideas the best."*
>
> —Sandra Harris, Founder and CEO, ECOlunchbox

What started out as mentoring from me has turned to a heightened exchange of ideas. We have shared trade show booths at different expos, market insights, and sales figures; co-marketed through our channels; and invited other like brands to join us. By joining together to expand our market category, we have lifted our brands in a very welcoming and profitable way.

Protect Your Brand

Now I don't want to leave you with too rosy a picture of co-opetition. There can be dark clouds filled with unethical bumps, and suddenly the relationship may shift and you find not only your products being manufactured elsewhere but your ideas co-opted. In our case, our most popular products were knocked off.

Another company was selling reusable eco goods and it was a simple decision to work with them, at first because they weren't making anything. Their business was focused on building a web platform, aggregating multiple products in the reusable category to ride the wave of consumer demand. By being on their more user-friendly website, our brand gained a wider audience.

We expanded our brand presence on their platform so customers could easily find us. However, as popularity for our styles grew, the company requested we private label for them, replacing our branding with theirs on our products. When we declined, they stopped selling our brand. Instead, they copied and began manufacturing and selling our styles themselves. They went with a "business as usual" approach, putting profits ahead of partnership. That company eventually sold to a much larger corporate brand and we remain independent. It's a path with many roads, and when you're a Tiny Business you get to choose which one you want to take.

In cases like that, it is essential you are prepared to act. Do everything to legally protect your brand. Defending your brand can take a lot of resources, so instead of being thrown off course every time another business "steals" an idea or product, be ready to respond with all the right forms and practices.

I will say, though, we live in a world where making something for less somewhere else is easily done. What matters more than your product being copied is your brand integrity and its reach. The bigger focus needs to be on protecting your brand. That's where your energy and vigilance as a Tiny Business needs to go. You can't build an impenetrable wall around your brand to protect it, but you can build a moat that will make it easier to defend what you've built.

Exercise: Prepare to Protect Your Brand by All Means Possible

Here's my exhaustive list. Start checking off items today!

♦ Get everything in writing.
♦ Register your brand name in multiple permutations, word and design marks (We registered Eco-Bags, Eco-Bag, ECOBAGS, ECOBAG).

◆ Register your brand with multiple uses. Be accurate for what you're doing now and what you may intend to do in the near future. Cover your bases.

◆ Work with an intellectual property lawyer to have all your ducks in a row.

◆ Have a strong brand "cease and desist" letter on hand to use when needed. Set up a Google Alert for all uses of your mark on the web.

And if you find a business using your intellectual property (IP):

1. Reach out to them, copying your IP lawyer on every communication. (Confirm with your lawyer that no action is needed unless you request it. This way you don't incur legal fees but the recipient of your communication takes you seriously.)

2. If the business responds amicably, thank them. I've found that 80 percent of businesses will respond positively and respect your request. And maybe they actually want to be in a relationship with your business and sell the authentic brand. Congratulations, you've made a new partner!

3. If they are not responsive, fire off those IP and cease-and-desist letters and keep all correspondence and supporting documents filed accurately. Take all the steps and go as far as you legally can to get them to remove all occurrences of your brand on all marketing and communications.

Parting Thoughts

You're never above the forces of the economy—or the market. It's an obvious point but one that needs additional focus for your Tiny Business. You can casually listen to the radio or a podcast or you can actively listen and take a deeper dive. You need to determine for you what sound waves have the potentiality to disrupt your focus and intentions. I'm not suggesting hysteria; in fact I'm suggesting the opposite.

66

Don't freak out. Figure it out.

99

Have a well-thought-out approach in place before things go south so that you calmly dissect what you're hearing and determine how it could impact your organization. Get your numbers in order from the start (more on that in the next chapter). Then use your Tiny Business priorities to guide your decisions with more confidence and intention and less stress.

Chapter Six

Tiny Business Is
Lean Business

"
*I don't care if you think you're
a math person or not.*
"

As a business owner, you need to be intimate with your numbers. Even if you have a bookkeeper, an accountant, and a CFO.

Generally, the bookkeeper keeps it all organized, the accountant makes sure you're in compliance with taxes and helps with strategies, and your CFO does forecasting and budgets. Despite all that capable backup, you still need to know the numbers like the back of your hand.

With almost three decades in business, I still speak entrepreneur more than I do numbers. But I know my numbers. That is because the lifeblood of my business is cash flow.

Cash is the log in the campfire and the gas (or electricity) in the car. Without cash, you can't do what you need. Too much cash and you may do things you don't need. I've been in both positions and you'll likely find yourself in both too. Let me just say that having too much cash isn't a real problem until you run out and don't have a reserve. But having too little cash will exhaust and stress you out.

Mac McCabe has consulted and held senior management positions with national brands such as L.L.Bean and Greyston Bakery. For the last few years, he has been my go-to financial guy and forecaster.

We met at a Social Venture Institute[1] event in the Hudson Valley where I was invited to talk. And since that fateful meeting over cauliflower casserole we've been connected at the hip. (Truth be told, Mac could've been a key resource when we were spiraling down in the recession, but moving forward . . .)

What's happened since working with Mac is that Eco-Bag Products' business decisions are made based on forecasts and margins. Cash-based, informed responses have 99 percent replaced reactions and we're so much better off for it. That's why I asked Mac to bring his expertise to this chapter.

From Mac's accounting and numbers perspective, Tiny Business means taking a lean, minimalist approach to getting maximum results. Surviving and thriving is all about the numbers. If you are only passionate about your "why" and you don't care about the numbers, then there is a genuine risk that your venture will not survive.

In his words:

"Tiny businesses are still businesses. They all exist on a competitive playing field where some will succeed and many will fail. Who succeeds? I don't

have a crystal ball but I do know that if you understand your numbers and how those numbers impact results, you will almost always improve your odds for success. And I also know that even if you have an instant hit in spite of flying blind, sooner or later you will get into trouble if you don't know how your business operates numerically."

To build a business within reach of what you want, you must keep it within reach of reality. This chapter is all about how to do what I didn't do at first but that I do now. Largely because of Mac, who helped me to really get to know my numbers.

Cash Flow and Access to Cash

What's enough cash flow? What's your baseline? Whatever the number is, it should be tied directly to your level of confidence with sales and expenses, based on history, with projections and unknowns gathered through relationships you make and nurture. So much of running and building any business comes in the bits and pieces of information you gather in formal and casual exchanges. You can't know everything, but you can know enough to make a decision or know where you need to go to get help.

The big key to cash flow is knowing and mapping out all your known expenses—typical and atypical, current and x months—in advance against a forecast with historical figures. When you start you may not have a history to reference,

If you feel like this . . .

66

. . . you need cash and a strong financial structure and network or else you'll fail.

99

which is why it's important to work with an accountant or have conversations with others in businesses like yours.

The ideal cash flow position is having enough cash to:

- ◆ Do what you need to do.
- ◆ Allocate a percentage to what you want to do.
- ◆ Have a safety reserve left over for just in case.[2]

Cash on hand is where the rubber meets the road. My initial experience was with bootstrapping, using my own cash and taking out credit cards. I invested $2,000 of my own savings and used low- and no-interest credit cards to buy inventory and cover overhead. I managed the credit cards with a spreadsheet, negotiating extensions and flipping cards when the interest rates were about to go up. I had about $100,000 out on credit cards with cash advances and never paid more than 2 percent interest on any balance.

The credit card rules here were simple:

◆ I paid off all credit card balances in full every month OR . . .

◆ If the interest rates were low and I had to, I carried the balance, scheduling payments monthly and always paying more than the minimum.

◆ I used the credit cards for essential business needs only, and they never left my office.

Over the course of eighteen long years I bootstrapped and created a market. I grew slow and steady, which gave me plenty of time to enjoy my growing family. I worked regular business hours. It was only after grossing $3 million and seeing my business going into a free fall during the recession that I looked to secure backup money.

Luckily, I had already started talks with my banker and got an SBA (Small Business Administration) loan[3] when the recession hit. I had also refinanced my house to pull cash out just in case the SBA money wasn't enough. This was before we could get a credit line big enough with a favorable rate.

Since I bootstrapped, I worked 100 percent for myself, but I realize not all businesses can be built like this. If you want or need to build a business faster or you do not have personal funds, you will need to raise money with investors or crowdfund. What I caution about raising money is that it can be a huge distraction, taking a lot of time away from the actual running of your business.

You have to find the right investors because once you take their money, you are working for them or, in the best of situations, with them as partners. Different types of investors measure and expect different returns (e.g., traditional venture capitalists versus angel investors).

Although I don't have direct experience with these approaches, I know someone through the Social Venture Network who does: Jenny Kassan, attorney, capital-raising coach, and author of *Raise Capital On Your Own Terms*. She has made it her mission—and her business—to help businesses more efficiently and effectively get funding. I encourage you to read her book to get a better understanding of the capital-raising landscape and the wide array of options open to you.

The Importance of Good Credit

You need good credit in business. Simply stated, you need to prove you understand how to borrow and repay by having a history of doing so. You are being watched when you use financial tools such as credit cards. This is money being "loaned" to you by an institution or company. You want to use these tools to the best of your ability—that is, borrowing money and paying it back according to the stated terms—so that you can establish good credit. Prompt and systematic payments and keeping your balances in line with your overall assets are what make you a good credit risk.

I'm personally not a big fan of loans, SBA loans included, because they can hamper your cash flow. Sometimes, however, you cannot get a credit line until a bank has seen you manage a loan. Therefore, it is essential to build excellent credit with loans and credit cards. Do this before you need the money—before you are in a hole.

A credit line is now my preferred financial product because it is flexible. Unlike loans, you can adjust the repayment, borrowing and repaying according to the ebb and flow of the business. Once you are able to get a credit line, take a conservative approach. Only borrow what's needed for payables in the next one or two weeks and then repay as soon as you can. This shows the credit line being used again and again and demonstrates credit worthiness. Once you build a good credit rating, you can get access to more cash with different products.

Credit and loans can be a lifesaver and a business opportunity when used appropriately. But never think of this cash as your own. It's not.

66

If you owe money, ultimately, it owns you until it is paid off.

99

Accounting: Use It Every Day and Use It Well

If you're anything like me, you're not naturally inclined to work in the abstract world of numbers—especially when there are so many exciting things to do like products to create, customers to meet, and logos and websites to design. But, as Mac warns, procrastinating on your numbers is as dangerous as driving without your headlights at night.

And that's where a well-designed chart of accounts and reports comes in . . .

Accounting is a tool to track and record your everyday financial reality, including:

- ◆ How much money was actually received for the sales that were made.
- ◆ How much the items that you sell really cost to make or purchase from others.
- ◆ How much you paid for rent, utilities, marketing, travel, insurance, and payroll (including all those benefits and taxes).

It can tell you how you are doing, what's working, and what isn't. It can also help you to watch trends and patterns so you don't get surprised when you arrive at work one day and find out:

- ◆ Your bank account is overdrawn.
- ◆ You're going to miss payroll.
- ◆ Your most important customer hasn't paid you in two months.

"

Brush your teeth, do the dishes, keep your accounting current.[4]

"

It is so important to have your books in order with every transaction put into the right account—how else can you know where you have been and where you are going? In the next section, I'll explain why knowing those two things is so important.

Forecasting and Financial Reports: Where Have You Been? Where Are You Going?

Comparing your current financial results against past years is interesting to track, but it's not good enough. Prior to each new year, you need to put together a monthly plan of where you see yourself going. The best way to do this is to lay out a projected monthly income statement (often called a pro forma) and have a line for every revenue and expense that you track in your accounting system.

Next, you need to measure what actually happens each month against your forecast. If you see that the numbers are not as rosy as your forecast, do something! Find out why your sales are lower, or your cost of goods is higher, or your utility bill is sky high. It may just be timing or it may be a problem. And if it's a problem, keeping check on a monthly basis will allow you to take action before it becomes an even bigger, possibly insurmountable problem.

"

If you don't take charge of your numbers,
sooner or later your numbers will rule you.

"

80/20 as an Operating Guideline

In chapter 3, I introduced the Pareto principle, which states that 80 percent of results are produced from 20 percent of efforts. Applied to the numbers side of things, it can mean that:

- ◆ 20 percent of your customers make 80 percent of purchases.
- ◆ 20 percent of your product items result in 80 percent of sales.
- ◆ 20 percent of your advertising delivers 80 percent of results.

So why is this good to know?

Mac gives this example:

Several years ago, I stepped in to help a midsize wholesale distributor in the natural products business that was in a cash crunch. Early on, I called in the purchasing manager and asked about his department's process for ordering (in the food category you replenish as often as once a week). He proudly said that he had a very organized system where his team had vendors that were divided up by days of the week and the buyers ordered on those days with no real regard for the volume, the vendor, or indeed each product.

The company sold 6,000 items, and I told him that he should put more effort into managing the 1,200

(20 percent) that brought in most of the revenue. He thought I was crazy. Nevertheless, a very clever IT manager wrote a quick program that ranked each item by sales. The result: the cumulative total somewhere between the 1,150th and 1,250th items generated 80 percent of the total sales.

So how did this help me? I immediately told the purchasing manager to buy an extra 10 percent reserve of each of the top 20 percent items and cut back on reserves of everything else.

Sales increased because they were never out of stock of the key items, and total inventory went down because they weren't carrying so much of the slow movers that eventually went out of date. The increased sales and fewer expired goods that resulted were the first steps to getting them out of the hole.

Exercise: 80/20 Your Tiny Business

Dive deep into your books to learn:

✦ Who are your top 20 percent of customers? How do you make sure they are kept happy?

✦ What are the products or services you provide that bring in 80 percent of your sales ("the significant few")? How do you ensure you're never out of them?

✦ What are the items that will have no impact if you run out ("the insignificant many")? Can you cut back on inventory of these products?

✦ Which marketing endeavors bring in the best results (80 percent)? How can you concentrate your efforts on refining these initiatives?

✦ Is there a geographical cluster where your best customers live? And how can you find more customers there or in similar locations?

Mac's example clearly illustrates the importance of a strategy built on concentrating on "the significant few" and not "the insignificant many." The key is to look at your own business through the 80/20 lens and see what you learn.

Tiny Business Metrics: Are You Living Up to Your "Why"?

In addition to managing your cash and growing profit, as a Tiny Business owner you have other key things to measure around how you want to be in business (your "why").

It's important to check in and measure how you're doing with your personal and professional priorities on a weekly, if not daily basis. It's easy and normal to get thrown off course.

For example, it's easy to make a commitment to "fair wages for fair labor" from a comfy office, possibly thousands of miles away from your manufacturer, and then reap the benefits through effective marketing. But to be true to your Tiny Business values, you need to establish relationships on both a personal and professional level with your partners and make sure you are on the same page. You have to see how they do business with your own eyes and use measurements and third-party certifications to ensure promises are being kept. The bottom line is you have to establish trust *and* metrics.

Establish criteria to meet your Tiny values and measure the criteria. One great (and free) resource is the

"Maybe try blowing on it?"

B Corp Measure What Matters assessment to help you measure your impact on society and the environment.

> **66**
> *"Maybe try" is not an effective strategy to put the wind in your sails—or your sales.*
> **99**

Get crystal clear on the numbers that matter to your Tiny Business—like your cash flow, your performance against your forecasts, and any metrics you use to help you stay true to your "why." Then lead consistently with those metrics front and center for all your employees to embrace. You may have started the business but your team is responsible for running it, so make sure the culture supports their efforts.

By clearly articulating your "why," you will guide the day-to-day "how" of your Tiny Business.

Breathe—and Thrive

aka Get a Glass of Water!

Chapter Seven

Walk to Work
(Even If You Work from Home)

"
*Being an entrepreneur is
an endurance sport.*
"

You need to always be in training so that you can improve on the past and be prepared for the future. You are accountable to you 100 percent of the time. Your job is to bring your best self forward every day.

As an entrepreneur and business owner, you make a lot of decisions and keep a lot of balls in the air. It's important you don't get stuck in a rut, attempting to fix a new problem with an old approach. Staying out of ruts takes training. As someone asked at a retreat I attended:

"How can you create the future if you are referencing the past? You will only re-create the past in the future."

I'm not suggesting you forget the past. There are lessons to be learned from it, of course. The future, however, has the possibility to look different, to be something we haven't thought of yet, to become something new. Staying fresh and open to new ideas is part of being on top of your game.

That's why you need to regularly exercise your mind and your body.

Science shows, as if we even need to be told, that sitting at a desk all day is not good for you. Duh! It's not only bad for your back, it's not good for your head. Neither is doing any kind of repetitive action. How can you possibly be creative and effective as a business owner by doing the same things in the same way from the same position every day? You can't. I'm not talking about your work systems here that are required efficiencies. I'm talking about the bigger picture—the thinking required to keep you and your business healthy.

The importance of regularly getting up, moving and stretching, breathing air into your lungs from a different part of the building or neighborhood, and hydrating with water cannot be overemphasized.

66

Go get a glass of water.
(You'll have to stand up!)

99

Make exercising your mind and body part of your schedule. It doesn't happen magically, but you can find "magic" and ease if you practice regularly. And, by the way, you should encourage these practices with your employees. This is how you reduce workplace stress and avoid burnout.

Here are some of my proven methods for keeping your mind, body, and Tiny Business healthy.

Don't Think Outside the Box, Think Outside

I walk to and from my office (twenty minutes each way) with my dog most days. My office and home are close together, and the route is walker-friendly. I planned it that way.

Steps matter. You can always fit steps in. Whether you work in your home or an office, make it your business to walk at least twenty minutes every day before you start your workday. See if you can find time during your day and then preferably afterward too. Walk around the parking lot. Walk up and down stairs. Challenge yourself with different terrain. If you take mass transit, get off a few stops early and walk the rest of the way. The benefit from these walks will outweigh all the reasons you can find for not doing it.

Schedule Meetings with Yourself

When you call it a "date," it's personal; when you call it a "meeting," it's business. It's your business to take care of yourself.

I've had a longstanding "meeting" with myself at my local pool for more than sixteen years, three to five times a week. It's in the middle of the day and it's nonnegotiable. It's a business meeting that gets added to my office calendar for all to see with an "out of office" time block. It means coordinating other business activity around it unless something is so urgent that it absolutely takes precedence. It's no secret to my staff that I leave to swim midday either. I return to the office with wet hair!

Make It a Team Activity.

If you're taking someone out for lunch or a coffee, walk the long way there! Or have a walking meeting outside. This is how you model healthy living and set an example for your team. Although you can't make someone get up and take a walk, if they do they will be healthier and your business will be healthier because of it.

Change Your Patterns—Step by Step.

Your brain grows when you provide new and different experiences but, as we all know, change is hard. Closely examining your relationship to change is essential to building a Tiny Business.

Change is hard because it feels insurmountable. Culture will have us believe that you are required to do the whole thing at once and if you fail you won't be any better off than when you started. Untrue. All you have to do is pick one direction and take one step at a time.

I climbed Angels Landing at Zion National Park, gaining 1448 feet of elevation using chains hand over hand to reach the top view. I wasn't alone; there were hundreds of us climbing the cliff shear step by precipitous step.

But there were many more people at the bottom watching, deciding if they wanted to take the risk of hiking up with the chains. Be honest with yourself: Which group do you choose to be part of?

Choose a New Habit

If you're feeling stuck in your old ways, start a new habit. The best way to get out of a practice that may be hindering you is to replace it with a new one that is enjoyable and rewarding.[1]

A friend gave me a sand timer as a gift. I loved how the sand expired after exactly twenty minutes. I was bored and looking to reengage a sense of curiosity in my life, so I decided to use the timer to shift me.

I began to write for exactly twenty minutes a day, every day, for a year. I sat in the same chair, turned the timer over, and wrote about whatever came to my mind. The subject didn't matter; putting words on paper did. It wasn't easy and at times was very uncomfortable.

When the timer finished, I stopped—even if I was mid-sentence. Keeping to exactly twenty minutes was important even though sometimes I wanted to continue to write. By limiting my writing time I stimulated an interest, piqued my curiosity, and created a desire to write more. Instead of giving myself more than my allotted time, I learned to be very efficient with it. It's that old saying, "If you want something done, give it to a busy person."

When I started writing every day, I didn't have any outcome in mind other than doing something new. Somehow, I managed to write a few short stories, begin a full-length play, and start the book you are reading now. (I did, however, expand my time commitment to finish writing it.)

Tune In, Turn Off

Allow yourself free time. Whether it's walking to and from the office or sitting at the local coffee shop, give yourself space between commitments. Don't fill it with phone calls, podcasts, or the news. Savor it and create a mini personal retreat in the middle (or beginning or end) of your day. Many brief, unattended moments when added together will give you energy and improve your listening and ability to focus. Silence, when you intentionally turn off devices, will serve your decision-making executive functions and your nerves.

66

Your cell phone is part of your tool kit. Use it with discipline.

99

Go Away

"Tune in, turn off."
—Kenny Gellerman, Co-Founder,
Enterprise Training Solutions

This is a big one. Vacations are essential to your well-being and effectiveness as an entrepreneur. Put your vacation time on your personal and work calendars with as much notice as possible. Make plans, go, and don't look back.

When you have to travel for business, make it an adventure. Don't cram your schedule and then rush back to the office. Take days in front of or after conferences to de-stress and wander aimlessly.

If you think your business will suffer or, worse, fail because you go on a vacation with your family, you need to rethink and restructure. If you believe anyone in your organization cannot take a vacation because it will put you in jeopardy, you need to restructure.

66

A Tiny Business is about building something agile and profitable, on your own terms, so that you (and your team) can be home for dinner.

99

Actually, the best way to test the strength of your organization is to go away and not check in. Chances are you'll return to find it humming along and, if not, at least you'll be in a more relaxed and ready state to address next steps.

"Did you remember to mail that check?"

Your job as owner is to provide leadership and insights, not manage. With the right people working with you, stepping away gives them the opportunity to shine, to build their problem-solving skills, find opportunities, and stretch themselves.

Exercise: Plan Your Next Vacation

Planning is your best defense against interruptions. Here's how:

- ◆ Review all pending projects and build your vacation into the schedule.
- ◆ Create wide margins around any project (especially IT) and allow a bumper of two to four weeks on any project, because you don't want to be on an island somewhere, with limited Wi-Fi, fixing a problem from the corner of a bathroom (the only place with a good signal). Clearly, I'm speaking from experience.

- Connect with partners and clients you generally speak with at this same time of year a few weeks ahead of time. Set their expectations so they know they can talk to you now or when you return.

- Create a contact plan for just in case—that's the 20 percent of cases where you're the last resort to call if anything occurs.

- Create "away" messages that give alternate contacts for problem solving.

- Personalize your away message to specify you are:

  ▶ off the grid

  ▶ unplugged

  ▶ enjoying time with your family

  ▶ inspiring others to do the same

- Create a "WELCOME HOME" message and leave it in your office or on your desktop so it's the first thing you see when you return. Welcome yourself back before you dive into work.

And here's my rule for responding to messages when I take a week off:

If I get it on a Monday or Tuesday and it's important, I'll respond.

If I get it on Wednesday or later, well, who can't wait until the following Monday? Really?

Make up your own rule and follow it.

Quit

There are two types of quitting:

1. **Quit for the day, at the end of the day.** You're tired, so go home or close your computer if you're already home. Stop looking at emails. Stop working!

2. **Quit your business.** You are burned out and can't possibly suffer another week of doing what you're doing—even though you're doing what you want to do on your own terms.

I highly suggest Quitting (with a capital Q) your business at least once a year—perhaps in a fit of rage. Take the time to quit—thoughtfully, though.

- ◆ Make a list of all the things you want that you are not getting or achieving.
- ◆ Find your ideal job or jobs that will allow you to achieve those things.
- ◆ Rewrite your resume.
- ◆ Send it out, along with cover letters.
- ◆ Actually go on interviews.

That's right—see what it feels like to leave your business, dressed for an interview. Go through all the steps and watch your thoughts as you do this. You will get extraordinary insights into who you are and what you value as important whether you take the new position, restructure the one you're in, or return to what you have as is.

I quit in frustration around year seven of my business. It must've been that seven-year itch. I found a job, prepared my resume, and got an interview. I was confident I could land any job I wanted. But as soon as I got to the gigantic office park, my heart rate sped up and my stomach signaled to me, "Run away as fast as you can . . . RUN AWAY!"

I ignored my physical signs and went into the bland, freezing lobby, found the elevator, and proceeded to the office on the ninth floor. No one looked happy to be there.

I took a deep breath and walked out of that windowless room within twenty minutes of arriving and went straight back to Eco-Bags Products with a new sense of what I wanted and how I could make it happen.

If, unlike me, you do decide to capital-Q QUIT . . .

66

Here's how to make your business work for you (whether you're in it or not).

99

A Tiny Business is a scalable, tangible asset that you have options with. You can:

- ◆ Sell and walk away.

- ◆ Sell and stay on in some capacity (if your future professional life is linked to the brand, there's no reason to lose the leverage on what you've built).

- ◆ Find a partner and work side by side.

- ◆ Find a partner to run the business and become a silent stakeholder.

- ◆ Continue to own 100 percent and not participate by hiring a CEO and putting key metrics, goals, and reviews in place.

- ◆ Sell to your employees.

66

It can run without you, but can it grow?

99

This is the question to look at if you are deciding whether to move on in some form. Tiny Businesses do need to keep growing to be sustainable. Old customers fall away and new customers must come in. It's an ebb and flow. And, there's the ecosystem—your employees, suppliers, and customers—to consider. Your relationships will affect the decision you make.

Build your own formula, using three key elements:

◆ Your intuition

◆ Your accountant

◆ Your lawyer

Identifying the knowns and playing them out in "what-if" scenarios with levelheaded professionals will support your intuition—this has been my experience after thirty years in business. All the things I think I know need to be challenged again to see if I'm being honest with myself. Make the decision slowly.

66

Rash decisions are called as such because they can leave an unseemly mark.

99

Chapter Eight

Share Your Tiny Story

Don't Fall into the Trap of Isolating Yourself

When you do what you do for a period of time, keeping true to your Tiny values and achieving some success along the way, you will eventually get noticed—especially if you keep up with relationships. That's when it's important to share your story.

As an entrepreneur, you will always have stories to tell and there will always be someone who can benefit. We live in a world where we think everyone knows, or owns, more than we do. Some do. Some don't.

Share what you've learned. It is an act of generosity, and it is as simple as sending the elevator back down or holding the door open for the next person.

> *"Send the elevator back down."*
>
> —Lee Eiferman, LeeWords

Share to Shape the Future

Speak whenever you are invited. Look for opportunities to share and mentor. Regularly schedule time in your week to guide or coach someone who requests help. This is you making a donation, helping to shape the future.

A Brownie Girl Scout troop came to visit my office recently. They were doing an eco-project and one of the moms is married to Joe, our UPS delivery guy. Into our quiet office came eighteen boisterous Brownies more interested in talking than listening. I talked about business and the environment. It was a forty-five-minute whirlwind and I had no idea what they got out of it or didn't.

The next day, I received an excited call from the troop leader letting me know that on the way home, they stopped to get snacks and said, "No plastic bags, thanks," to the shop owner. A few days after that, I got word they created and signed a pledge to stop using plastic bags. A few days after that, I got an envelope filled with effusive thank-you notes from every child. Amazing. These girls are our future.

One time, Yale University invited me to speak to their School of Management. Thirty-five years ago I tried to go to Yale. I auditioned there to be part of their acting program. I didn't get in. Now, Yale was inviting me to speak to their graduate class of environmental entrepreneurs. Me.

Even students at one of the world's most prestigious universities connected to my stories. What resonated was my humble beginning, starting from scratch as an actor, and making it past a million dollars with a business that impacted culture. They were nervous and excited, about to step out to make their mark, just like I was over three decades ago. Those who came up to me expressed their thanks for sharing my story. They had a sense that if I did it, so could they.

Share to Connect

When I get invited to speak, it's not the facts or figures that stick. Whether it's new entrepreneurs, graduate students, or middle-school kids, it's the stories that resonate. And while happy endings are always great to talk about, what everyone really wants to hear about is the adversity, the failures, the pickles we get ourselves into. How we navigate the challenges of solving a problem. How we create and run a business to solve that problem. How we risk, fail, and risk again.

> *"Risk. Fail. Risk again."*
> —National Theater Institute,
> Eugene O'Neill Theater Center

Connection is what happens when you make your audience laugh (or cry). Connection is what spurs them to their own aha moments. It is what inspires. We live in a hero myth culture. We want to align ourselves with others who have what we aspire to have and embody what we aspire to be. Even a glimmer can open the door to new possibilities.

It's important to be generous and share what you've learned if you've learned a thing or two. Even if your business failed, talk about it. Talk about why it failed and what you know now that you didn't know then. You're not offering advice, you're sharing a story, and stories can have a direct impact on another human's psyche.

119

Volunteer with your expertise on nonprofit and community boards. Share your perspective. Do it for the experience; don't be attached to the outcome. If you can offer even the smallest piece of wisdom or stir a pot of dullness, you will have made a difference. Don't hold back what you've learned.

There's No Place Like Home

Draw a fifty-mile radius around where you live or work. Wherever it is, you can be sure there are enlightened, engaged, and generous people in the circle you just drew. I bet you will find a local or regional library, chamber of commerce, Lions or Rotary Club, high school, and a community college or university. These provide abundant opportunities for you to offer your stories and share your insights. If not, create the event or meet-up yourself.

Don't do this in order to get something back. Go to give back, to share stories of your experiences, to become a part of the community fabric.

I realized, just a few years ago, that my town is a gold mine of interconnected people. I live in metro New York, surrounded by educated, engaged, and connected folks. But I spent so much time looking farther away for what I needed, I didn't look next door. My next-door neighbor and I always spent our time talking about our kids. But once we turned our attention to our work, we found we had even more to share and support each other with—plus we expanded our network tenfold.[1]

I was probably over twenty-two years into running my business when I realized, quite literally, there's no place like home. I woke up and opened my eyes to see that in my immediate group of friends, family, and neighbors, there was not only a wealth of expertise and connections but that I, too, had things to contribute.

I stopped listening for what I needed and started listening to what other folks needed. I listened to learn instead of listening to get. And when I expanded the idea of community, my circle of "associates" widened, as did my comfort with people within in it.

❝

Life (and business) is incremental.

❞

That's one of the lessons I learned from training for Climate Ride.[2] Every decision matters, yet no single decision matters more than the next (most of the time). If you want to go somewhere, you first have to get in the car, put gas in it, start the engine, and head in a direction. You get there one mile at a time. Just keep on moving.

Just keep your Tiny Business moving.

There is time for reflection and process at the end of the day. Why is it always at the end of the day? Maybe that's just the process. Maybe there's time in the middle of the day if you make it. Go outside and sit in the grass. Read a book with your dog in the midday sun. Get a glass of water. I swim—not always, but often, and in the summer, every day. It's magical. It's the magic of Tiny Business.

Go outside and sit in the grass.

Notes

Chapter 1

1. Free writing is when you sit down to write with the goal of getting something—anything—on paper. Spelling and grammar don't matter. No edits allowed. It helps to break through mind blocks and get to the heart of what you may be thinking or feeling about a certain subject.

Chapter 2

1. B Corps are for-profit companies certified by the nonprofit B Lab to meet rigorous standards of social and environmental performance, accountability, and transparency. Today, there is a growing community of more than 2,100 Certified B Corps from 50 countries and over 130 industries working together toward 1 unifying goal: to redefine success in business.

Chapter 3

1. Of course, there are always exceptions and ours was Stanley. To gain access to NYC shoppers at the newly opened Union Square greenmarket we were told that all sales had to go through Stanley, a senior citizen who made his way from Harlem every Saturday and Wednesday to the market to sell nonfood items. At Union Square Market we would be reaching early adopters of farm to table goods, our perfect tribe of trend leaders. By working with Stanley, who everyone loved, we got the best market research ever. Plus, he knew how to sell ECOBAGS!

    With Stanley's help and our entrée into the natural products industry, we found our tribe and I found more of me.

Chapter 4

1. A touchpoint is a point of distribution and can be a person or business.

Chapter 5

1. Guido, by the way, visited the office every year, around the holidays, to deliver chocolates. He lived in Switzerland and New York City and had big clients all over the world, and we, by all measures, were his only tiny customer.

Chapter 6

1. If one of your Tiny Business priorities is to leave the world better than the way you found it, you may be interested in Social Venture Network (SVN), the parent organization for SVI. SVN is a nonprofit membership organization whose mission is to "support and empower diverse, innovative leaders who leverage business to serve the greater good." You have to meet certain criteria to join, but it's a worthwhile organization that you should be aware of as you grow your business.

2. From the very beginning of your business, you need to have a cash reserve. Banks are more likely to loan you money (and offer you an increase with a better rate) when you have money than when you don't have money. Whether you're starting your business with your own money or with raised or borrowed funds, pick a percentage from every transaction and put it into your "reserve capital" fund. Do not use it for anything until you know it can be replenished or backed up by a credit line or low-interest source.

3. SBA loans are provided under programs offered by the U.S. Small Business Administration to tailor to the specific capital needs of growing businesses. See https://www.sba .gov/funding-programs/loans.

4. Mac McCabe, Sustainable Business Consultant

Chapter 7

1. See "Neuroscience Insight: How to Break Bad Habits" at the Chopra Center website: http://www.chopra.com /articles/neuroscience-insight-how-to-break-bad-habits.

Chapter 8

1. That's a whole other topic—the one about how women talk, or don't talk, about business. How we go to the heart of what matters—family, health, vacations—instead of diving into work. Work is the thing that occupies most of our time, yet we hardly talk about that when we're together. In fact, we hardly know what each of us does on a day-to-day basis.

   I personally believe if women talked about our work and passions more, we'd find a gold mine. What if we shifted our conversations to what we do and how we can work together and play together in that sandbox? It could be revolutionary.

2. Climate Ride is a nonprofit organization that organizes life-changing charitable events to raise awareness and support sustainability, active transportation, and environmental causes.

Resources

B Corps
https://www.bcorporation.net

B Impact Assessment
https://beta.bimpactassessment.net/get-started

Raise Capital On Your Own Terms: How to Fund Your Business without Selling Your Soul by Jenny Kassan
http://www.jennykassan.com/raisecapitalbook/

Rotary International
https://www.rotary.org

Social Venture Institutes
http://svn.org/attend-an-event/social-venture-institutes

Social Venture Network
http://svn.org/

Women Presidents' Organization
https://www.womenpresidentsorg.com/

Women's Enterprise Development Center (WEDC)
https://wedcbiz.org/

Index

Index

Acknowledgments

I have been fortunate to be supported and inspired by so many. From learning the ropes of retail in our family store, Milt's Army and Navy, with parents Joan and Milton to talking "shop" with my real life sisters; "tiny" entrepreneurs, Ellen Ornato cofounder of The Bolder Company and Heidi Feldman cofounder of Martha's Vineyard Sea Salt.

My husband, Blake, and children, Julian and Eva, inspired my "why." I wanted to spend time with family and make a living doing work that mattered with a socially responsible "how"—big goals for starting a "tiny" business in 1989. Blake gets an extra callout for being super patient, the wires beneath my desk (aka IT support), for naming the business and brand, and for making music that fills my soul.

Early acting training taught me about listening and failing. Thanks to the places I studied: Clark University, the Eugene O'Neill Theater Center at the National Theater Institute, acting and improvisation in DC and New York City, and decades on the Pavalon floor at The Noyes School of Rhythm, where connecting to your inner dancer is celebrated.

Building a brand is one thing. Making it thrive day-to-day is another. Many thanks to Andrew Dyer, who keeps it together with intelligence and grace; and to Susan

Askew, Mollie Nalven, and Alex D'Attore; Lisa Pavlik, Christina O'Reilly, and Susan Ujadowski; and others who have passed through our doors.

It's all about community. Thanks to my peers in the Women Presidents' Organization where we share what we know . . . and don't know: Linda Price, Carrie O'Donnell, Tammy Jersey, Gayle Lob, Cathy Jirak, Emily McKhann, Joan Landorf, Beth Dempsey, Maryann Donovan, Sandra Ruiz-Desai, Mary Jaensch, Kathleen Perkal, Deb Volansky, Nancy Yale, Ann Buivid, and Lucie Voves. And a big shout out to people like Rose Penelope Yee, Tim Yee, Lara Pearson, Corey Blake, and so many others who are members of B-Corporation and Social Venture Network. Those two business communities are what keep my fires burning.

Seth Godin brought together an amazing and powerful group of women entrepreneurs ten years ago for a program he called FeMBA. We're all still deeply connected and supportive of each other. Thank you to Seth Godin, Julie Burstein, Susan Danziger, Dahna Goldstein, Rebecca Rodscog, Desiree Vargas Wrigley, Emily McInnes, Nicole Gammon, Liz Forkin Bohannon, Jessica Lawrence Quinn, and Brooks Bell.

Editorial Director Neal Maillet saw the spark and encouraged me to write about the development of my tiny idea. Thanks to Neal and everyone on the talented and supportive Berrett-Koehler Publishing team: Steve Piersanti, Kristin Frantz, Katie Sheehan, Liz McKellar, Michael Crowley, Jeevan Sivasubram, and many others.

I didn't know how many stages a book goes through. I do now! Thanks to all who helped this newbie author on her first book journey: My sister, Ellen Ornato, who first called my business "tiny"; Jeffrey Davis, of Tracking Wonder Quest, who added the "magic"; Michael Boyce whose "start cold" approach is in my heart; Lee Eiferman of Lee-Words who laughed with me over the first draft and then coached me to find my narrative and workflow; and to Danielle Goodman, my developmental editor, who has skills I am in awe of. Thanks to Tessa Bell for the long walks while I marinated the concept; Kaja Gam, Ken Skalski, Hugh Locke, April Freeman, Trudy Ebanks Mindy Kerman, Kenny Gellerman; Debby, Tom, and Jennifer Boyce; Susan Davidson, Dave Thompson, Ellen Prior, and Mark Morganelli for being; Flip Brown for the introduction to BK; Mac McCabe for generously contributing his time and wit; and AnnMarie Nieves of PR Red for friendship and knowing how to move the needle.

I wrote this book because Deb Volansky, a friend in the Women's President Organization and owner of Connex International, kept saying "you're my inspiration" and I couldn't see how that could possibly be. I want to thank Deb for starting me on my inquiry, initiating the deeper dive into my "why," to articulate what has informed and driven me. My goal is to inspire and support. Let me know if I do.

About the Author

Sharon Rowe is the CEO of Eco-Bags Products, Inc., which she founded in 1989. In 2010, the company became a certified B Corporation.

ECOBAGS is the original reusable bag brand. Sold worldwide, it is recognized as "Best for the World" by B Corporation for social and environmental commitments and standards.

Sharon is a thought leader in social innovation and sustainable and responsible production. She speaks regularly on building profitable mission- and value-aligned businesses. Sharon believes that business is a currency for ideas that shape culture and can be used as a force for good. Her speaking engagements have taken her wide and far—from Yale University to Sing Sing Prison and from the Nairobi Center for Innovation in Kenya to the Social Venture Institute conference in the Hudson Valley.

She has been featured in *Time, Glamour, Entrepreneur,* and the *Wall Street Journal*; on NPR's Air America; and in the award-winning documentary *Bag It.* ECOBAGS were also featured on *The Oprah Winfrey Show*'s first Earth Day episode in 2007.

Sharon has received numerous awards, including the 2012 Enterprising Women of the Year, CBS Radio Women's Achievement, Westchester Business Council Entrepreneur of the Year, *914Inc.-Westchester* magazine Most Accomplished Women, the Women's Enterprise Development Center's Lillian Vernon Award, and the Westchester Collaborative Theater's Most Valuable Player.

Sharon is an active member of the Social Venture Network and the Women Presidents' Organization. She has served on the Hudson River Sloop Clearwater board and is on the Westchester Collaborative Theater board.

Sharon lives in the Hudson Valley with her husband, Blake, a musician and teacher. Her two grown children, Eva and Julian, are living out of state, pursuing their interests. Eva, a civil engineer, is focused on sustainable design. Julian, a cartoonist published in the *New Yorker*, contributed to this book.

Julian Rowe is a cartoonist from earth who's work occasionally appears in the New Yorker magazine. He lives on a small sailboat with his wife and two dogs.

Berrett–Koehler
Publishers

Berrett-Koehler is an independent publisher dedicated to an ambitious mission: *Connecting people and ideas to create a world that works for all.*

We believe that the solutions to the world's problems will come from all of us, working at all levels: in our organizations, in our society, and in our own lives. Our BK Business books help people make their organizations more humane, democratic, diverse, and effective (we don't think there's any contradiction there). Our BK Currents books offer pathways to creating a more just, equitable, and sustainable society. Our BK Life books help people create positive change in their lives and align their personal practices with their aspirations for a better world.

All of our books are designed to bring people seeking positive change together around the ideas that empower them to see and shape the world in a new way.

And we strive to practice what we preach. At the core of our approach is Stewardship, a deep sense of responsibility to administer the company for the benefit of all of our stakeholder groups including authors, customers, employees, investors, service providers, and the communities and environment around us. Everything we do is built around this and our other key values of quality, partnership, inclusion, and sustainability.

This is why we are both a B-Corporation and a California Benefit Corporation—a certification and a for-profit legal status that require us to adhere to the highest standards for corporate, social, and environmental performance.

We are grateful to our readers, authors, and other friends of the company who consider themselves to be part of the BK Community. We hope that you, too, will join us in our mission.

A BK Business Book

We hope you enjoy this BK Business book. BK Business books pioneer new leadership and management practices and socially responsible approaches to business. They are designed to provide you with groundbreaking and practical tools to transform your work and organizations while upholding the triple bottom line of people, planet, and profits. High-five!

To find out more, visit **www.bkconnection.com**.

Berrett–Koehler Publishers

Berrett-Koehler is an independent publisher dedicated to an ambitious mission: *Connecting people and ideas to create a world that works for all.*

We believe that the solutions to the world's problems will come from all of us, working at all levels: in our organizations, in our society, and in our own lives. Our BK Business books help people make their organizations more humane, democratic, diverse, and effective (we don't think there's any contradiction there). Our BK Currents books offer pathways to creating a more just, equitable, and sustainable society. Our BK Life books help people create positive change in their lives and align their personal practices with their aspirations for a better world.

All of our books are designed to bring people seeking positive change together around the ideas that empower them to see and shape the world in a new way.

And we strive to practice what we preach. At the core of our approach is Stewardship, a deep sense of responsibility to administer the company for the benefit of all of our stakeholder groups including authors, customers, employees, investors, service providers, and the communities and environment around us. Everything we do is built around this and our other key values of quality, partnership, inclusion, and sustainability.

This is why we are both a B-Corporation and a California Benefit Corporation—a certification and a for-profit legal status that require us to adhere to the highest standards for corporate, social, and environmental performance.

We are grateful to our readers, authors, and other friends of the company who consider themselves to be part of the BK Community. We hope that you, too, will join us in our mission.

A BK Business Book

We hope you enjoy this BK Business book. BK Business books pioneer new leadership and management practices and socially responsible approaches to business. They are designed to provide you with groundbreaking and practical tools to transform your work and organizations while upholding the triple bottom line of people, planet, and profits. High-five!

To find out more, visit **www.bkconnection.com.**

MIX
From responsible sources
FSC® C113845